"Steve McVey writes like a man .... is a true brother of the cloud of witnesses, determined to give us clear eyes to see and open hearts to know the endless, cascading, goodness and love of Jesus's Father. Thank God McVey left a paper trail."

C. Baxter Kruger
author of *The Great Dance, Across All Worlds*,
and the international bestseller *The Shack Revisited*

"Steve McVey has written a wonderful book for anyone who wants to delve deeper into God's grace. If you're looking for help because God seems to be both for us and against us, equally angry and loving, this book is for you. Interwoven with his own journey, Steve shows with biblical clarity how God is not split into two minds about us. Rather, a proper consideration of all of Scripture coupled with the best interpretive practices shows us that God is like Jesus Christ all the way down. Highly recommended."

Joseph Tkach
president, Grace Communion International
board member, National Association of Evangelicals

"The most important question we can ever ask is, who is God? And in the light of the answer to that, we then ask, who am I? In this book you will find simple yet profound answers to both questions. Steve has faced every question and difficulty head-on, leaving no stone unturned and leading the reader to the fullness of life in relationship with the holy Trinity through Christ. He challenges many commonly accepted ideas, and even if you have long agreed with the truths revealed here, they will come alive with new light. This is your best book, Steve, and a must-read for everyone!"

Malcolm Smith
founder, Unconditional Love International
author of *Power of the Blood Covenant*

"What if you knew that God is not angry with you? What if the God who *is* love is beyond anger? How would this inform and reform our ideas of sin and salvation, the cross and redemption, heaven and hell? Steve McVey 'goes there.' He is both bold and careful. Bold because the Father's heart of love and saving act of grace are firmly rooted in Steve's own heart and message. And careful because nothing here is mere novelty or sentimentalism—his gospel is rooted deeply in the text of Scripture, and his research in the early church fathers. He holds high the finished work of Christ and the importance of our response to it. Biblically sound, theologically orthodox—what we have here is the beautiful gospel of a grace-based, Christ-centered faith that draws out our 'yes' to God's 'yes.'"

Brad Jersak
Westminster Theological Centre
author of *Can You Hear Me? Tuning In to the God Who Speaks*

"Steve McVey is brilliantly gifted to engage his audience not only by sharing his own honest journey of discovery but also by leading us to the very source within us, where mere glimpses of the Father, Son, and Spirit's goodness become the feast that our hearts have been anticipating all along.

"In *Beyond an Angry God*, he brings simple clarity to the logic of God's theology—not merely by disarming distorted doctrinal ideas but by winning hearts to explore for themselves the immeasurable dimensions of the love of the Father Son and Spirit.

"In a world where multitudes feel unwanted, unloved, and unimportant, Steve introduces us to the heartbeat of creation—the fact that you are what inspires God most! You began in His most intimate thought!"

Francois Du Toit
author, *The Mirror Bible*

beyond an Angry GOD

Steve McVey

HARVEST HOUSE PUBLISHERS
EUGENE, OREGON

BEYOND AN ANGRY GOD
Copyright © 2014 by Steve McVey
Published by Harvest House Publishers
Eugene, Oregon 97402
www.harvesthousepublishers.com

Library of Congress Cataloging-in-Publication Data
  McVey, Steve
  Beyond an angry God / Steve McVey.
    pages cm
  ISBN 978-0-7369-5982-7 (pbk.)
  ISBN 978-0-7369-5983-4 (eBook)
  1. God (Christianity) 2. Spirituality—Christianity. I. Title.
  BT103.M38 2014
  231'.6—dc23

                                                        2014004002

Printed in the United States of America

14 15 16 17 18 19 20 21 22 / VP-CD / 10 9 8 7 6 5 4 3 2

To my grandchildren—
Hannah, Jonathan, Jeremy, Gabriel,
and even those grandchildren yet unborn—
let us live to enjoy and share
our Abba's amazing grace
through our very presence here
because in the end, that's all that matters.

Acknowledgments

Beyond an Angry God is the result of how God's Spirit has led my thoughts over the past nine years, and it reflects my own growth in grace. Countless hours of Bible study and prayer have gone into this book. Above all, I want to thank the Teacher, who came to guide us into all truth. The Holy Spirit never ceases to amaze me as He carries me forward along this journey.

He has spoken to me through many people and has used them to inform my thinking about the things written here. I'm particularly grateful to...

Baxter Kruger, whose book *The Great Dance* opened my eyes to a concept of God that I had never even considered and launched me on another leg of my continuing journey into grace. Baxter caused me to see that grace is even bigger than I had thought.

Mike Feazell's online program *You're Included* brought one theologian after another into my life, including but not limited to Elmer Colyer, David Torrance, Andrew Purves, George Hunsinger, Gary Deddo, Jeff McSwain, John McKenna, Gordon Fee, Paul Molnar, Ray Anderson, and Trevor Hart. The collective influence of these men on me has been astonishing.

Brad Jersak's insights into divine justice and the atonement rocked my doctrinal world.

Malcolm Smith's teaching on the unconditional love of our Father has nurtured me for two decades. In my opinion, there may be no better Bible teacher than him alive today.

Wm. Paul Young enabled this "Mc" to meet his Papa in a profound way, just as another Mac did in Paul's book *The Shack*. I thank God for how He has used Paul to renew a worldwide discussion of our Father's loving nature and for how his writing and teaching have touched me.

The influence of Grace Communion International stands as a testament to what grace can do at the corporate level of church life, and it has motivated me greatly. My heart resonates and rejoices with this modern-day miracle that moved from cult status to being one of the purest corporate expressions of truth and grace that I know.

If you see the fingerprints of those I've mentioned here in this book, you'll know it's because of the influence they have had on me in my journey. I've internalized and personalized so much of what they have taught that I'm not sure anymore about who said what. I appreciate and applaud them all.

I'm indebted to our Grace Walk team, spread across seven countries. I am thrilled to work together with them in sharing the wonderful message of Divine Agape. It has been exhilarating to see how He has led us forward together in this grace walk. I know how our Father works through them to encourage others, but nobody has been blessed by the Grace Walk team the way I have. I can't imagine ministry without them.

Special thanks goes to Gene Skinner, my editor for this book. His affirmation and input have helped sharpen and refine the message I share here in a way that has greatly improved it.

I'm grateful for my critics, who have caused me to question my views, resulting in praying and studying more as I examined and reexamined the things I've written about here. Iron sharpens iron, but stones can sharpen iron too. Thank you.

I'm thankful to friends online and in person who have offered words of encouragement, which often came just when I felt vulnerable and needed an affirming word. The names are too many to list here, but if you've affirmed the direction I have traveled, I'm talking about you.

My highest acknowledgement for people who affect me will always be reserved for my wife, Melanie. She has consistently encouraged, counseled, and loved me for more than 40 years. There is no face in this world in which I see Jesus more clearly than hers.

Finally, all praise to the Father, Son, and Holy Spirit, who have caused me to experience the joy of participation in the divine life in a way that theological words and concepts could never capture and experience can never deny. May He be glorified through everything written in these pages.

Contents

Foreword
by Wm. Paul Young

Many of us have read a book a second or third or tenth time and expressed, "Wow, I totally missed that before!" or "I didn't even remember that was in there!" The book itself didn't change—the same words are in the same order and often on the same page—so why the surprise?

It is because we changed. We moved. It is you and I who travel, walking around this mountain of words and looking at it from different perspectives. Perhaps the first time you were in the valley, looking at peaks massive and dominating your perspective. But this time you were high up on another range, looking back at that same mountain, catching a glimpse of where it sits as part of a larger landscape. Or maybe you have since journeyed around to the backside and stopped to view it from an entirely new vantage point. The mountain is the mountain, but we moved, we journeyed, we changed. True change happens at the pace and integration of our whole being. The heart is sometimes the first to see, but the mind with all its preconceptions and paradigms is the fortress, the final frontier, in which transformational change occurs, and even then only with our participation and permission.

Steve McVey has been writing "mountain guide-books" for years, directing and encouraging less intrepid explorers to journey with thoughtful expectancy, to comprehend and appreciate wonders of God's expression of truth in Jesus and truth in Scripture with eyes touched and opened by the Holy Spirit. He has also drawn our attention to the pitfalls and crevasses that often delay or damage our adventures. Over the years, Steve may have already taken you along a climb out of religious legalism and into the high places of grace. Now you may wonder about new change, new understandings, trails that lead *into* the mountain and perhaps to treasures long hidden and mysterious.

In this book Steve is not exploring a new mountain, but points of perspective that may initially seem startling or unexpected. There is a sense that he is no longer satisfied with the breathtaking panoramas and waterfalls that may have been hidden in valleys and gorges as one looks from a distance. McVey wants to know what this massive presence consists of—what is below the surface, why it stands with such authority and power—and he wants you to be part of the investigating community. Our Teacher is the Holy Spirit, our Guide especially in the subterranean and foundational, which holds and sustains our assurance in the veracity of our experience. We learn and explore and question within community, which originates inside the relationship of the Father, Son, and Spirit and is expressed outwardly into our one-to-another life.

Have we come to a mountain that cannot be touched, to a blazing fire, to darkness, gloom and a whirlwind? Who is this God? This matters, if for no other reason than this: The character of our humanity will be stamped with the nature of the God in whom we believe. A time is coming, and now is, for us to stop seeing the anger and fury of God in imagery projected from the darkened imaginations of our own damaged brokenness and disappointed petulance at best, and from the judicial retributive and punitive machinations of the ultimate narcissistic moral perfectionist at worst.

What if the revelation in Jesus opens our eyes to see that what we had thought was Mount Sinai was really Mount Zion? *Beyond an Angry God* will open your eyes to that reality.

Wm. Paul Young
author of the international bestsellers
The Shack and *Cross Roads*

Introduction

What if we have it all wrong about God? What if we've spent our lives seeing Him in one way when in reality, the deity we imagine is nothing like our God? Imagine leaving this world and meeting Him face-to-face only to discover that He isn't at all like we've been told. What if our well-intended but misguided religious education has contaminated our understanding of who God really is and has left us with a perspective about Him that hardly resembles the Father whom Jesus came to reveal? Can you imagine such a thing?

I can because that has already happened to me. I know now I had it wrong for a very long time, and I know I'm not alone.

I've been a follower of Jesus Christ since I was a boy. I was reared in a committed Christian home and grew up in church. After I left home I received a thorough education in a Christian university and seminary. I was a local church pastor for almost 21 years. Since leaving the pastorate and entering an itinerate ministry, I've taught the Bible on six continents and been in more denominational church settings than

I can count. I've seen the broad spectrum of the Christian faith across the world. The many Christian denominations that exist have a lot of differences, but they share at least one thing in common. It's the way they see God. Like me, many believers have had it wrong. Our prevalent opinion about God is polluted.

Seeing God as He Is

This contaminated concept of God has incapacitated us in our own grace walk and hampered our sincere efforts to see other people come to know and follow Christ. We've meant well, but we've tried to sell something that doesn't need to be sold if He is properly understood. The fragrance of authentic grace is an aphrodisiac for the human heart that's longing for love. The great spiritual need in the world today is for our eyes to be opened to see Him as He really is, not as sterile religion has portrayed Him to be or as the god our murky imaginations have conjured into existence.

When Jesus came into this world, the religious crowd of His day had a big problem with the way He talked about the Father. The things He said and the way He portrayed Almighty God's attitude and actions toward us stood in stark contrast to their understanding of who God is and what He thinks and does. It didn't just seem wrong to them. It seemed heretical, even blasphemous.

Faulty concepts about our Father linger today. I don't think it is accidental or incidental. The enemy of our souls wants nothing more than for us to totally misunderstand who God is. From the moment he caused Adam and Eve to become afraid of God in the Garden of Eden after they had eaten the forbidden fruit until today, his greatest weapon of mass destruction is to deceive people into having a wrong perception of God and how He sees and relates to us.

Is God *That* Good?

Sadly, the gatekeepers of this false paradigm are often religious leaders. Having been one myself and known many others, I know of what I speak. Had somebody told me the things I will tell you in this book while I was a local pastor, I would have thought they had lost their mind. I would have resisted the idea that God could be *that* good, largely because I didn't realize at the time that love isn't just one aspect of His character but is His fundamental essence. Love isn't one facet of God that stands on par with other divine attributes. Every feature of who He is must run through the sieve of divine agape, or it will be a misrepresentation of His character.

If God is part love and part something else—whether it be wrath or justice or anything else that we might imagine would stand in contrast to love—then we cannot legitimately say that He *is* love. Loving, perhaps, but not pure love personified. How could pure love produce anything that contradicted love? The mixture would render it impure. Our God is pure love personified, and everything about Him must be understood from that vantage point. No consideration of any subject related to Him should be excluded from that.

Growing in Grace

If you have read some of my writings from past years, you will discover that I say some things differently these days. This is the seventeenth book I've written or cowritten over a 20-year period. During those years, God's grace hasn't grown, but my understanding certainly has. That's one challenge with writing books—when the author grows, the things he has already written stay the same. This fact bothered me initially as I thought about writing this book, but I finally realized that I can either write from where I am today and trust that our Father will empower faithful readers to grow with me on this journey, or I can stagnate as a person and as an author. Integrity necessitated that I choose the former.

I was 40 when I wrote *Grace Walk*, and I'm 60 now. Our Father continues to use that bestselling book to encourage and help people all over the world. Some would say to leave well enough alone, but I pray this book will illustrate the title of that first book. Growing in grace is a walk, not a homestead where we set up residence so we never have to move forward again. What a tragedy it would have been if I had not grown in the past 20 years!

Much of what I wrote in my earlier books lays a foundation for the things you will read in these pages. But if you have been on this grace walk with me since the beginning, you will see the evolution I've experienced, and my prayer is that you will experience it too. Many of my readers have told me that they want to grow more, to go deeper in their understanding of grace. That is an admirable desire and one I hope we possess forever.

When we've gone as far as we can go along the path of grace in this life, when we reach the end of the road in this small space–time dimension and step across into eternity, at that moment we will surely stand in awe. For even though we will feel as if we have already traveled a great distance, we will see that we've only reached the first mile marker along the glorious grace highway that stretches into infinity. Then we will spend eternity moving still further and further into the experience and understanding of this wonderful grace.

Growing things change, and that includes people. If any of us still believe exactly the way we have always believed, one might be justified in asking if we have grown at all. In 1990, the Teacher began to reveal grace to me in a way I had never known it, and since then my journey has been exhilarating. I am thankful for my theological struggles and emotional upheavals as He dragged me deeper into the river of grace despite my fears. When we confidently believe what we believe, it can be a real challenge to recognize and acknowledge that we may not have it all right.

A Stretch

As I wrote this book, I knew it would likely stretch you. I pray your understanding of the vastness of your Abba's love will be stretched beyond where it is at this moment. I share what C.S. Lewis called "the author's fear" when he quoted his mentor, the renowned author George MacDonald: "If I mistake, he will forgive me. I do not fear him; I fear only lest, able to see and write these things, I should fail of witnessing and myself be, after all, a castaway—no king but a talker; no disciple of Jesus, ready to go with him to the death, but an arguer about the truth."[1]

My prayer is that as we journey together through this book, the Holy Spirit—the One who Jesus promised would guide us into all truth—will cause us to repent where necessary. To a great extent this is a book about *repentance*, a word that literally means, "to change our minds." That is what has happened to me, and my prayer is that it will happen to you too.

This isn't intended to be an academic book. I will present theological perspectives on various topics that will be founded in the Scriptures and developed by many theologians throughout church history. You may readily embrace the truths in this book. But if you have a long relationship to denominational traditions that contradict some things here, you may grapple with these truths before embracing them. I know I did.

I write with simplicity, having the pastoral goal of reaching typical folks who buy books at Christian bookstores because they want to be encouraged and to learn. Many renowned and scholarly theologians, both contemporary and historic, share the perspective from which I write, but I am not writing for the academic. If you are looking for an in-depth scholarly treatise, the bibliography may be of help. For my part, I offer this pastoral exhortation with the prayer that it will bring the average person who is hungry to know his Father more intimately into a deeper, conscious participation in divine agape.

If that describes you, I believe you will find this book to be both enlightening and encouraging. The truths here may even completely change your life. That's what happened to me as the Father taught them to me. I do warn you, however, that to journey into a deeper experience of your Father's loving grace, you might need to rethink some things you have believed. You'll likely need to change your mind about a few things.

Robert Capon described the challenge of rebuilding our theological framework.

> Whenever someone attempts to introduce a radically differ-
> ent insight to people whose minds have been formed by an
> old and well-worked-out way of thinking, he or she is up
> against an obstacle. Jesus said, their taste for the old wine is
> so well established that they invariably prefer it to the new.

More than that, the new wine, still fermenting, seems to them so obviously and dangerously full of power that they will not even consider putting it into their old and fragile wineskins.

But now try to see the point of the biblical imagery of wine-making a little more abstractly. The new insight is always at odds with the old way of looking at things. Even if the teacher's audience were to try earnestly to take it in, the only intellectual devices they would have to pick it up with are the categories of the old system with which it conflicts. Hence the teacher's problem: if he leaves in his teaching a single significant scrap of the old system, they, by their very effort to understand, will go to that scrap rather than to the point he is making and, having done that, will understand the new only insofar as it can be made to agree with the old—which is, not at all.[2]

I hope you will ask the One who Jesus promised will guide you into all truth to direct your thoughts as you read. Don't take my word for it, but don't take the word of those from whom you have been taught in the past either. It's a dangerous thing to be gullible. The Bible warns about being "carried about by every wind of doctrine" (see Ephesians 4:14). But an equal danger is that the truth of God be invalidated by the traditions that have been handed down (see Mark 7:13). I think that happens in the modern church much more than we recognize. Compare what you read here with what the Bible says and ask the Teacher to guide you.

The Lens of Love

The change in my own life over the past years has been remarkable. As a result of understanding our Father's love in a broader way, my relationship to Him has become more meaningful than ever. I love Him more. I love others more. I love the Scripture more. Love—that seems to be the pervasive force that has changed me and replaced the lens through which I see all of life now. I closely identify with Karl Barth's description of his own journey.

If I now attempt to judge how far I have actually changed in these last ten years with regard to my work, then it seems possible to put the case in a formula: I have been occupied approximately equally with the *deepening* and the *application* of that knowledge which, in its main channels, I had gained before. Both these developments have, of course, gone forward at the same time.[3]

I've been teaching the grace of God for many years, and as time passes I have seen my own thinking mature and have watched my understanding of grace change from a sunrise into the midday sun. What I saw in seminal form in the past, I am now seeing in its more matured state. I feel like Lucy must have felt in C.S. Lewis's *Prince Caspian* when she and Aslan spoke.

"Aslan," said Lucy, "you're bigger."

"That is because you are older, little one," answered he.

"Not because you are?"

"I am not. But every year you grow, you will find me bigger."[4]

The grace of God will continually appear to become bigger and more beautiful as we grow. Grace is the expression of Love Himself, and since He is infinite, it seems reasonable to assume that we will spend time and eternity discovering more and more about the vastness of the subject. Will we ever cross the finish line when it comes to knowing grace? Will we ever graduate and be able to rest in our current knowledge with confidence that we have finally reached the sum of the matter and there is no more? I certainly don't think so.

A Perfect Revelation of God

This development in my own life and ministry has led me to believe more strongly than I ever have that Jesus Christ is the source and center of everything we can know about our Father. He is the *exact* expression of our God and has left out nothing that we need to know about

Him (see Hebrews 1:3). If He had, no claim could truthfully be made that He was the perfect revelation of His Father. As you will see, this viewpoint is a guiding force in what I've written here. Bringing Jesus Christ to the center of my understanding of theology has been the catalyst for unprecedented change in my perspective. Barth described this growth in his own life.

> The positive factor in the new development was this: in these years I had to learn that Christian doctrine, if it is to merit its name and if it is to build up the Christian church in the world as she must needs be built up, has to be exclusively and conclusively the doctrine of Jesus Christ—of Jesus Christ as the living Word of God spoken to us men. If I look back from this point on my earlier studies, I may well ask myself how it ever came about that I did not learn this much sooner and accordingly speak it out. How slow is man, above all when the most important things are at stake![5]

I believe some important things are at stake in the contemporary church. The starting place for rightly understanding those things is theology—what we believe about God. The word *theology* comes from *theos*, which means "God," and *logos*, which refers to a word that expresses a concept or idea. Surely, our concept of God must be the starting point because it will inform our beliefs about every other biblical topic. From that place we will begin with confidence that His Spirit will renew our minds to the truth of His overwhelming goodness and love.

Chapter 1

Grace Is a Dance

I begin this book with an embarrassing confession. I can't believe I'm going to admit this, and even worse, I can't believe there was a time when I actually saw God this way. One thing is certain—when you understand how severely distorted my concept of God was for a long time, there will be no doubt in your mind that He can transform anybody's perspective. That's the only reason I'm willing to admit it.

I used to see God as a petty deity who just sat around waiting for somebody else to offend Him. He wasn't looking for trouble, but trouble just seemed to find Him because we humans could do no better than bumbling our way through life, messing up again and again. In my perception, considering who He is and what He expects of us, how could He *not* become agitated or even angry with me since I kept failing to consistently live the godly lifestyle He expected? This misunderstanding of God shaped how I perceived life at the deepest level. That's true for all of us—the way we perceive God affects everything else in our lives.

Anytime something went wrong for me, I tended to immediately scrutinize myself to see what I'd done that would cause God to let such a thing happen. One day, as I walked toward my car to go to work, I noticed I had a flat tire.

I knew I shouldn't have skipped my quiet time this morning, I thought.

I know, it's pathetic. Sometimes when one of my children misbehaved, I'd think, *God is letting this happen to show me what happens when I don't consistently pray and read the Bible with my family.*

Maybe I would have a financial challenge—the car would break down or the washing machine would quit working—and I would think, *I should have given more money for missions. Now God will take His money this way.*

Yes, it is embarrassing to admit now, but I saw God as a temperamental, petty, easily offended God who wouldn't hesitate to show me His displeasure when I didn't live up to what He expected from me. I know now that I saw Him as volatile. He was ready to bless me in a great way if I did the right things, but He would not hesitate to let life collapse all around me if I didn't do what He expected me to do. I wouldn't say I saw Him as mean. I just saw Him as being so holy that He couldn't let my shortcomings lie without allowing something to happen to wake me up and move me toward a better performance. It's like seeing a smudge of dirt on your white shirt. You *have to* wipe it off, or it will stand out so much that you can see nothing else. Well, my shirt was plenty smudged, and I kept the Divine Wiper busy.

What Is God Like?

Sadly, I've seen that many people share the perception I had of God's character and personality. Maybe you haven't been so far gone as to believe that God would let you have a flat tire simply because you didn't have your quiet time. But my earlier legalistic foolishness highlights the importance of our understanding of God's nature. Is He a God whose attitude toward us at the moment depends on what we are or aren't doing? Is He given to anger and punishment when we don't do the things He wants us to do? When we look at the failures in our own lives and in the whole world and our inability to live the lifestyle we were all created to live, how could God not be angry most of the time? "All have sinned and fall short of the glory of God," the Bible tells us. If sin makes God angry, common sense would suggest that He must be mad a lot!

I raise the question again that I asked in the introduction because it is central to the message of this book—is it possible we really do have it wrong? Could it be that God isn't angry about the things going on in this world or in your life? Might He be different from what we've thought? What is this God like whom we claim to know and to serve? What can we know about Him? He is the one who stands over every detail of our lives—more than that, over every detail of everything that exists—so it seems that having a clear understanding of the kind of God He is would be helpful to say the least.

Before the Beginning

The Bible begins with the four simple words, "In the beginning God…" If we want to know this God, is there a better place to begin than the beginning? Actually, there is. To start *before* the beginning is wise if we want to understand who God is, why we are here, and what this life is all about. After all, our identity and our destiny don't find their roots in the finite, but in the Infinite One. If you think you can find your origin in Adam, you aren't looking back far enough. Your source is the One who set everything in motion in the beginning—the One who preceded that beginning. You weren't an impulsive idea your Creator had in time. He held you dearly in His heart before He spoke the first molecule into existence.

From the supergalactic to the subatomic, this space–time box in which we live is a small environment that resides in and is sustained by the One who created it. He stands outside this dimension and holds it in the palm of His nail-scarred hand. The wonder of wonders is that this small cosmic container is your Creator's special jewelry box because it contains one of His most precious gems—*you*.

Our God existed before there was anything else. "In the beginning God…" The first time He is mentioned, the Scriptures reveal an important facet of His nature. The Hebrew word translated *God* is

Elohiym. The word is plural—a noteworthy fact because it reveals that our Father doesn't abide alone. There is a plurality in His very essence.

Today, you and I understand that our triune God exists as three in one. We know all about the Father, Son, and Holy Spirit, but the concept of the Trinity hadn't yet been revealed when the first verse of the Bible was written. Our God's disclosure of Himself bloomed among us like a flower that gradually reveals its complete beauty only when it comes into full blossom.

The Israelites who read Genesis would have seen the plural word *Elohiym* but would certainly have missed the significance you and I can see in it today. They had no concept of a Trinity. The Jewish people have always recited the Shema—the central prayer in the Jewish siddur (prayer book) and often the first section of Scripture that a Jewish child learns. The core of the prayer are words from Deuteronomy 6:4: "Hear, O Israel! The LORD our God, the LORD is one!" The world of ancient Israel was polytheistic—the other nations and tribes believed in many gods. *Elohiym* disclosed Himself to Israel as the one and true living God. An intellectual understanding of the triune nature of that one God finally began to emerge with the Incarnation of Jesus. He said that He and His Father were one (see John 10:30) and that the Spirit would shortly come (see John 14:16-17) .

The word *Trinity* wasn't used until Tertullian coined the term in the late second century, but the concept of the Trinity is taught in the Bible from the very beginning. It is important to note that the very first verse of the Bible alludes to the threefold nature of our God. So it would seem then that based on the fact that this is the very first thing God reveals to us about Himself in the Holy Scriptures, the importance of the Trinity must be *big.*

Which God?

Our planet is more pluralistic today than at any time in history. On the other hand, we see many unique customs, cultures, and convictions merging together. When I was a child, each county and culture of the world had distinctive characteristics that plainly delineated it from the others. Those differences are becoming less and less evident today. The Internet, television, and the ease of travel from one side of the world to the other has caused much of global life to blend together, and syncretism (the merging of differing belief systems) seems to be the order of the day.

But one thing that isn't merging is the way we all perceive God. The word *god* elicits different meanings to different people. I remember speaking to a group of college students in China and mentioning Jesus Christ. They had never even heard His name and asked me who He is.

"He is the Son of God," I answered.

"Which god?" they replied.

That was an awakening for me. I'd used the word *God* all my life without realizing that other people understood it in a completely different way than I did. On another occasion, a young man in India told me he was fasting to his god, and as we talked, I discovered he was actually fasting to and worshipping Hanuman, the monkey god. Seriously—the man was fasting to a monkey!

So when we say *God*, we need to clarify what we mean by that. Even Christians have a foggy understanding of the word. Depending on where you grew up in church, chances are that your mind goes to one member of the Godhead while the others are marginalized. For instance, if you grew up in a liturgical church, like the Presbyterian or Episcopalian church, you probably think of the Father. If you grew up in a Baptist or Methodist church, you most likely think of the Son. If your roots are in the Pentecostal or Charismatic world, the emphasis was likely on the Spirit.

God Is a Relationship

God is a triune God. He exists as three in one. Understanding the Trinity is more important than many Christians realize. Why does it matter that He is triune? It matters because as three in one, our God is first and foremost relational. In the eternal realm, the Father, Son, and Spirit have always existed and forever will exist in a circle of intimate love.

John said, "God is love" (1 John 4:8). That is the most important thing that can be said about Him. When we speak of God, we speak of shared love. Unless we understand that, our concept of Him will be skewed or even totally twisted. The circle of divine love in heaven may be the most important thing we can grasp about God. That alone would sort out a lot of foolishness, such as what I admitted embracing when I was younger.

If this relational nature of God is the very first thing He chose to show us about Himself in Scripture, it must be central to how we see and understand Him. Though He is one being, He enjoys intimate interaction among the three persons of the Trinity. The biblical God is first and foremost a loving relationship. That defines Him, so everything we know about Him must fit within that definition.

Some people see the Father, Son, and Spirit as if they were three separate gods, but they aren't. That view is called tritheism, and the church renounced it as a heresy. Neither does God simply reveal Himself in three separate ways, just as I might present myself as a husband, a father, and a son. That approach is called modalism or Sabellianism, and the church renounced it too.

Another prominent heretical view of God during the early years of the church was called Arianism. Arius, a presbyter in the church at Alexandria, taught that since Jesus was the only begotten Son of God, there must have been a time when He didn't exist. Arius taught that God created Jesus and then endowed Him with divine attributes. Some cult groups still hold that view today.

The response of the church to that error was swift and strong. Another Alexandrian presbyter, Athanasius, defended the biblical teaching about the second person of the Godhead by stressing Jesus's deity as well as His humanity. In the year 325, early church leaders met in Nicaea (in modern-day Turkey) and affirmed Athanasius's position. Consequently, a confessional document now known as the Nicene Creed expresses the relationship among the members of the Godhead and includes these words about Jesus:

> We believe in one Lord, Jesus Christ,
>   the only Son of God,
>   eternally begotten of the Father,

God from God, Light from Light,
true God from true God,
begotten, not made,
of one Being with the Father.

It later says this about the third person of the Trinity:

We believe in the Holy Spirit, the Lord, the giver of life,
who proceeds from the Father [and the Son].
With the Father and the Son he is worshiped and glorified.
He has spoken through the Prophets.[1]

Don't skim past this creed because it represents an important part of church history. With it the church affirmed something important—very important. What was it? It was the affirmation of the union of the Father, Son, and Holy Spirit. Our God is a relational God who has eternally lived in a self-sustained communion of love and life existing within Himself. That defines God. Above everything else, He is all about communion, relationship, and interconnectedness—all based on love.

Do you believe this is true? Does the Bible indeed present God from the very beginning as One whose very essence exudes a shared love? It's important that you see this point now because it is the groundwork for things you'll discover in the chapters to come. The way you see God will affect everything.

Theology is simply what a person thinks and says about God. Whether you are aware of it or not, you have a theological position right now because you have a concept of God and what He is like. I pray that as you read this book, you will see God more and more as the pure love that He truly is.

You'll see that I don't get bogged down in microscopic theological details in these chapters. However, we do need to understand some foundational theological truths if we are to have a healthy, biblical, and joyful ongoing walk with our God. So before moving any further, embrace this first and foundational aspect of God's nature—He is relational. Hold on to that thought as you read this whole book.

As you will see in later chapters, this is critically important because many people see God as being primarily *judicial*. That is to say, they see Him as a Judge who is interested in our behavior before they see Him as a Father who is interested in *us*. That is a serious problem for those who hold that view because it leads to the faulty concept of an angry God who needs to be appeased in some way. As we will see, that is not the Father whom Jesus came to reveal.

The Divine Dance

From the corridors of eternity past, the Father, Son, and Spirit have always been perfectly fulfilled. Nothing has lacked in the perfect setting in which they live. They find great joy in each other and in the life they share. The Father loves the Son and the Spirit. The Son loves the Father and the Spirit. The Spirit loves the Father and the Son. The relationship among the Trinity has always been fulfilling, exhilarating, and satisfying in every way. God could have spent endless ages doing nothing more than enjoying Himself.

The Church Fathers used a Greek word to describe this special relationship—*perichoresis*. The word first appears in writing in the seventh century and refers to what some have called a "community of being" in which each person of the Trinity, while maintaining His distinctive identity, shares His very essence with the others. The word denotes a oneness that creates a unified movement of intimate relationship—like a dance.

Look again at the word *perichoresis*. It comes from the words *peri* and *chorein*. *Peri* denotes a circle, as in the word *perimeter*. *Chorein* means to make room for and to enclose. Dancing is a good metaphor for this loving, synchronized movement of the Father, Son, and Spirit enclosed together in one essence. Our God isn't a somber, rigid deity who sits in a frozen position on a divine throne, from where He scrutinizes and judges His creatures. It might be more accurate to describe Him as a divine Dancer who eternally celebrates love and life in the divine Circle Dance that is Himself.

C.S. Lewis affirmed the significance of this.

And that, by the way, is perhaps the most important difference between Christianity and all other religions: that in Christianity God is not a static thing—not even a person—but a dynamic, pulsating activity, a life, almost a kind of drama. Almost, if you will not think me irreverent, a kind of dance.[2]

Dancing Beyond Time

This divine dance exists outside of time and space in the eternal now. Time is an illusory phenomenon among human beings that appears to be sequential and measured by a succession of happenings. In the eternal realm, everything is simultaneous and all exists in "the now." There is no tomorrow to God. He doesn't wait in anticipation for anything to happen because He already knows it all at once. More to the point, He knows all people at once, and that includes you. There has never been a time when you were not known and treasured as precious to God.

God told Jeremiah, "Before I formed you in the womb I knew you" (Jeremiah 1:5). Later He told him, "I have loved you with an everlasting love" (Jeremiah 31:3). The word *everlasting* points not only toward an unending duration in the future but also to ancient times long ago. To be exact, it points to a state outside of time.

Long before your parents ever caught each other's eye, you were already loved. You were treasured in your God's heart. You didn't just show up on planet earth as the random result of physical intimacy between your mom and dad. The One who loved you when there was no such thing as time brought you forth into time. It was His joy to show you off to the world. The Father, Son, and Spirit must have clicked their heels in their joyful dance on the day you were born.

Why Are You Here?

Why did He bring you into existence? It was simply to be loved. The quality of love shared among the members of the Trinity has always been perfect. There is no way it could be improved. Divine love can be nothing less than perfect love.

In the beauty of the eternal plan, this love finds greater expression in quantity, not quality. The quality of love was impossible to enhance, but our wise God knew that the dance could be extended to include others, thus making it a shared experience beyond the Father, Son, and Spirit. That's where you come into the picture. Humanity was created to participate in the great dance. We did nothing to deserve to be included, but the fact that He has included us has beautifully expanded the dance of God into a dance of grace. Only a God who is pure love would do such a thing as that!

The Father, Son, and Spirit already knew and enjoyed a perfect relationship, so why else would He purpose to create a species with which He might share this love? What could possibly motivate Him to want to expand the circle? Love—that is the only possible reason. Our God is a selfless, generous, other-centered, giving God. He didn't need you. He *wanted* you!

My friend Francois Du Toit puts it well in his rendering of Ephesians 1:4-6 in *The Mirror Bible*.

> He associated us in Christ before the fall of the world! Jesus is God's mind made up about us! He always knew in his love that he would present us again face-to-face before him in blameless innocence. He is the architect of our design; his heart dream realized our coming of age in Christ. His grace-plan is to be celebrated: he greatly endeared us and highly favored us in Christ. His love for his Son is his love for us.[3]

You aren't simply a cog in the cosmic wheel. You are your Father's dream come true! The apostle Paul described us as "God's masterpiece" (Ephesians 2:10 NLT). You have been embraced and bound up in Jesus Christ and are now His very offspring (see Acts 17:28). You have been set in the place of a child who is loved and accepted by the Father just as surely as Jesus Himself knows that love and acceptance. Your place in the triune circle dance is as safe and secure as is the place of Jesus for the staggering reason that you are in Him.

The Word for You

If the news that God has always intended to include you in the circle of His trinitarian life seems too good to be true, consider this biblical witness: "In the beginning was the Word, and the Word was with God, and the Word was God" (John 1:1). The New Living Translation renders the verse, "In the beginning the Word already existed. The Word was with God, and the Word was God."

What is this Word that was already there at the moment the second hand ticked for the first time? You already know that the answer is Jesus. He was already there when the beginning took its first step into time. The biblical translators all know the verse is talking about Jesus. That's why they all capitalize *Word*.

But the question is, why is Jesus called the Word? To answer that, we must first define the meaning of the term itself. What is the meaning of *word*? It is the expressed embodiment of a concept conveyed from one person to another. In other words, it's the way something in one person's mind makes its way to the other person.

We know that the Father, Son, and Holy Spirit all share the same essence. They live in complete openness and transparency among themselves. None has to inform the others about things they don't know because they already all know.

So for Jesus to be identified as the Word who already existed at the beginning is very significant. A word exists for the purpose of communicating to another—but each person in the Godhead already fully knows everything the other persons know, so why did this Word exist in the beginning? If Jesus, as the Word, didn't need to communicate anything to the Father or the Spirit, to whom did He have something to communicate?

The answer is thrilling. The intended recipient of the Word is you. God had something He wanted to tell you before the first proton and neutron began to vibrate. What was this important news He arranged to tell you long before you were even here to tell? It is that He loves you, that He always has and always will. The fact that the Word was there from the very beginning, and the fact that there certainly was nothing

He needed to communicate in Himself among the persons of the Trinity, is the basis of this great gospel of love that has the power to transform the whole cosmos. Look back into the place before time began, and you'll find a loving God whose heart rejoiced at the thought of bringing you into existence so He could share His love with you.

Theologian (and my friend) Baxter Kruger makes this note:

> This decision flowing out of the being and character of God, this decision to share all that the Father, Son and Spirit are and have together with us, and the relentless determination that it would be so, is the true and proper context for the death of Jesus Christ. Jesus Christ died because the Father, Son and Spirit absolutely refused to go back on their dreams for us. "For God so loved the world," Jesus says, "that He gave His only Son…" (John 3:16). Before creation, the Triune God decided that the human race would be included in the Trinitarian circle of life and fullness and glory and joy. And with that decision came a fire in God's belly that it would be so no matter what it cost. The Lamb of God was slain indeed before the foundation of the world.[4]

Being Lost Is All Relative

Our God had an eternal dream that He would create you and bring you into the eternal circle of His love and life. That fulfillment of that dream initiated with Him, was activated by Him, is perpetuated by Him, and will be consummated by Him. The traditional language of the religious world speaks of finding God, but the truth is that He is the One who has found us!

In Luke 15, Jesus demonstrated this very fact. He spoke about the lost sheep, the lost coin, and the lost son. In each case, the word *lost* could be properly used only because each thing was already objectively connected to a place of belonging. A sheep that didn't already belong to a shepherd wouldn't be lost. It would simply be wild. A coin could be lost only if there was an owner to whom it belonged. The prodigal son was considered lost only because his home was with a father who had always known where his son's life was really rooted. Catherine Marshall wrote about this in her book *Beyond Ourselves*.

> Nothing can be lost that is not first owned. Just as a parent is compelled by civil law to be responsible for his family and his property, so the Creator—by His own divine law—is compelled to take care of the children He has created. And that means not only caring for the good children, but for the bad ones and lost ones as well. If a person is a "lost sinner" it only means that he is temporarily separated from the Good Shepherd who owns him. The Shepherd is bound by all duties of ownership to go after all those who are lost until they are found.[5]

The starting point for the sheep, the coin, and the prodigal wasn't their lostness but their *belonging*—despite their current status. In each case, their authentic identity was defined by their relationship to the one to whom they belonged. Notice that in these parables, Jesus never indicates that the shepherd of the lost sheep, the owner of the lost coin, or the father of the lost son were ever angry about the lostness of their treasured possession. Far from it. They were driven by a loving passion to recover what they loved—at any cost.

When the shepherd finds the sheep, "he calls together his friends and his neighbors, saying to them, 'Rejoice with me, for I have found *my* sheep which was lost!'" (Luke 15:6). When the woman lost the silver coin, she carefully searches her house. "And when she finds it, she calls her friends and neighbors together and says, 'Rejoice with me; I have found *my* lost coin'" (verse 9 NIV). When the father of the prodigal runs out to meet his son, falls on him, and hugs him, he calls out to his servants, "This son *of mine* was dead and is alive again; he was lost and is found" (verse 24 NIV).

Lostness has no meaning apart from the reference point of belonging. If belonging didn't come first, nothing could be lost. This is true not only with sheep, coins, and rebellious sons. It's true with humanity itself. Before we were ever lost in Adam, we already belonged in Christ.

Ephesians 1:4 is completely clear: "He [God the Father] chose us in Him [Jesus] before the foundation of the world." To be chosen in Him before the foundation of the world, we obviously had to *be* in His heart before the foundation of the world. You have always belonged. We all have. Always.

The Initiator

In a wonderful and pivotal demonstration of grace, our loving God took the initiative to deliver us from our lostness. Jesus identified His mission, saying, "For the Son of Man has come to seek and to save that which was lost" (Luke 19:10). To properly understand God's nature, it is important to realize that He doesn't wait for us to make a move to resolve our problem of sin. As Pure Love, He acts independently of what we do or don't do. When humanity wasn't seeking Him, He came looking for us! (See Romans 3:11.)

The lost sheep did not find its way home. The lost coin could not find its way home. The prodigal son would not find his way home. Sure, he came back to the house with a rote script he had prepared to garner a good meal and a warm bed, but it's totally possible to be at the house without really being home. He was truly home only after he gave up his silly notion that he needed to do something and he simply accepted his father's acceptance.

Our triune God's passion is to have us participate in the dance, and that passion is so strong that He left nothing to chance. "While we were yet sinners, Christ died for us," the apostle Paul explained (Romans 5:8). He didn't wait for us to ask for His help or even to be sorry.

A Heroic Rescue

A couple of years ago, two 24-year-olds—a man and woman— broke into an oil drilling company about an hour away from Dallas, Texas. Four containers filled with oil and water were on the property. About three in the morning, this young duo decided to take a cigarette break and thought one of the containers would be a good seat. You can imagine what happened next.

When the firefighters arrived, they extinguished the two burning burglars and threw a foam blanket over the other containers to keep the fire from spreading. They rushed the pair to the hospital, and their lives were saved. All this happened without so much as an apology or even a request for help from the foolish thieves.

Do you think our God would respond to mankind's dilemma any less heroically than these firefighters responded to the two burglars? The firefighters didn't even know the people they rescued, but God loves each of us. How much greater would His motivation to rescue us from disaster be? We were doomed in Adam, and our fate would have been eternal death for sure. Was God angry with us about that? No. To the contrary, He had already determined to remedy that situation and had always had a plan in place.

Athanasius, the Alexandrian church leader I mentioned at the beginning of this chapter, wrote about this as well.

> What, then, was God to do? What else could He possibly do, being God, but renew His Image in mankind, so that through it men might once more come to know Him? And how could this be done save by the coming of the very Image Himself, our Savior Jesus Christ? Men could not have done it, for are only made after them Image; nor could angels have done it, for they are not the images of God. The Word of God came in His own Person, because it was He alone, the Image of the Father, who could recreate man made after the Image.[6]

Pure Love would not, indeed could not, stand idly by while mankind withered away into death. Our triune God knew that man would sin in time, so He took the initiative and solved the problem in eternity even before there was any such thing as time! Good Friday wasn't a divine reaction to human sin. It was an eternal reality that existed long before it manifested itself on the human calendar. What had already been eternally determined in heaven finally materialized on earth, but it was simply an expression of something already settled long ago. *That* is the kind of God Jesus came to reveal!

God Is Love and...

God's love isn't predicated on our response. He loves because "God *is* love" (1 John 4:8). This aspect of God's nature is the benchmark from which we interpret everything else that can be known about Him. Is love simply one of God's characteristics? Or instead, does John's statement speak to the core essence of who He is? Are there other aspects of His nature that need to be seen in balance with the reality of His love? The answer is a resounding no.

Love is our God's DNA. "God is love" is the most definitive statement that can be said about Him. Some may think that to suggest that love is the defining factor of everything that can be known about Him is shortsighted and dangerous. They may argue that God has other aspects of His nature that need to be seen in balance with His love. In particular, many people point to His justice and wrath.

Critics contend that by focusing on His love to such an extent presents a lopsided view of who He is. In reality, their own viewpoint creates the exact problem they fear. Those who attempt to align justice, wrath, or any other divine qualities alongside His love as separate but equal realities malign His true nature. In chapter 5, I address the topics of justice and wrath, and you will see that even these can be understood by recognizing divine love as the fountainhead from which they flow.

Love isn't a part of the divine nature. It *is* His nature. Think of it like this. Imagine you're using a pie to illustrate God's essence. How would you show the places His love, justice, and wrath hold in His nature? Would you divide the pie into three equal pieces? Or would you have a very large piece of the pie signify His love and two smaller pieces represent His justice and wrath? How would you divide the love, justice, and wrath of God?

The fact is, such a division doesn't exist in God's divine nature. Instead, the entire piecrust is the love of God, and every other aspect of His nature is a piece of the pie. In other words, God's justice, wrath, holiness, sovereignty, and all the other traits that can be known about Him must be understood as parts of His love. Otherwise, God is part love and part something else.

Love is the pie — all the above traits compose the pie of love ~ coherency

Pure Love

does not hold water

If I handed you a glass of water and told you it was pure, you would assume nothing else was in the glass but pure water. If the glass contained anything other than water, even in small traces, I wouldn't be honest calling it pure water.

Is God pure love or not? Of course He is. If anything that contradicts love were present in Him, we couldn't truthfully say that He is pure love. We would have to say He is part love and part something else. The very idea is a scary thought.

What if God were part love, but other aspects of His character contrasted with love, as some theological constructs suggest? How would we know that at any given moment, we might see a side to God that we don't want to see? How could we ever rest in peace about our relationship to Him? How could we be sure that we would be only the objects of His love and not the targets of things that came from a place other than love? Can you imagine a deity dealing out something that didn't come from love? It's the kind of thing you might find in horror movies.

My whole life was revolutionized the day I sincerely and irrevocably believed that God is love. Until then, my confidence in the constant expression of His love could be so easily shaken. My circumstances occasionally made me wonder. Sometimes an Old Testament verse tripped me up and caused me to doubt. At other times I saw things going on in the world around me that I couldn't reconcile with the existence of a God who really is pure love.

The time came, however, when I put my eyes on Jesus. We have seen that He is the "exact representation of [the Father's] nature" (Hebrews 1:3). Because that is true, the question is, did Jesus leave out part of who His Father is? If He did, and if His Father has a dark side that Jesus didn't bother to mention or show us, that was a *big* omission! Reasonable people could even say it would have been dishonest to leave out such information while telling us, "He who has seen Me has seen the Father" (John 14:9). Jesus didn't do that. You can count on it. There is no other side to God that Jesus didn't reveal.

Don't let anything other than Jesus Himself be your source for understanding who the Father is. "God, after He spoke long ago to the fathers in the prophets in many portions and in many ways, in these last days has spoken to us in His Son, whom He appointed heir of all things, through whom also He made the world" (Hebrews 1:1-2). Even insights gained from the Bible are rightly understood only through Jesus. He came to show us the Father, and what He has shown us perfectly and clearly is that our Father is love. That's it—nothing more, nothing less.

When we focus exclusively on the love of God, when we see love as the totality of His being, are we leaving out something? To say yes is to insult Divine Agape. Love is His fundamental makeup. Everything that can be known of Him must be seen through the lens of agape, or we end up presenting a god with a multiple personality. Jesus proved that God is pure love by coming into this world.

The day came when "the Word became flesh, and dwelt among us" (John 1:14) to communicate this divine love, which would not be squelched. Rejection didn't still it. Death didn't stop it. Even hell couldn't stall it. The only thing left is for us to receive it—to receive *Him*.

The dance of God has become a dance of grace. The eternal melody of love that defined the Father, Son, and Spirit was never intended to be enjoyed only among the Trinity. The harmonious, transcendent beauty of the Great Composition was to sound forth from the boundless realm of eternity and enter a tiny room of space and time and, even more amazingly, enter into the individual hearts of beings within that room who were created for no other reason than to participate in that dance of love.

Chapter 2

Sin Is a Sour Note

Have you ever noticed a movie score building with intensity in a great drama as the plot reaches its most exciting moment? That's the way I imagine the scene when these words were spoken in the eternal realm: "Let us make human beings in our image, to be like ourselves" (Genesis 1:26 NLT). Those words were the culmination of an intention that, like its Source, had no beginning. With this statement, that generous purpose was fulfilled in those chosen from eternity past to be included in the divine embrace.

With a gentle, fragrant breath of love, humanity came to life in the paradise created for its pleasure. This world would be the ballroom in which human beings would participate in a grace waltz choreographed by their loving Partner. What was the first action their Creator would take toward them? Have you noted that important aspect of the Creator's relationship to those He created?

It seems logical to conclude that the first time God acted in any way toward those He created reveals much to us about Him and His intent for humanity. The God of all creation was about to interact with the man and woman He had brought forth from the dust and into whom He had breathed His very breath. What would that look like?

God's Heart for You

Consider this thrilling account in Genesis 1:27-28: "God created man in His own image, in the image of God He created him; male and female He created them. God blessed them…"

He blessed them! The moment Adam and Eve opened their eyes, their Creator blessed them. That action forever carries astounding implications for mankind. The heart of our Creator is to bless you. Dead religion presents a freakish caricature, a pseudo-god who is reluctant to bless his creatures unless they toe the line of impeccable moral behavior and tireless service to him. But the authentic God of the Bible blessed Adam and Eve immediately—before they worshipped, before they served, before they prayed, before they displayed any kind of action at all. This first divine act toward humanity tells us so very much about Him.

Love always takes the initiative without waiting to see what its recipient will do first. From the instant of mankind's creation, our God's blessings didn't depend on human service toward Him. God's grace certainly motivates us to honor Him with acts of service, but His blessings are not the slightest bit contingent on our service to Him.

Then the Bible goes into even greater detail in its description of the birth of mankind. The first thing He did was to bless them, but what was the first thing God *said* to them after He created them? He might have started by setting the ground rules for how they were to live. That would have made perfect sense to us, but that's not what He did. He might have told them they had an obligation to fulfill now that He had given them a paradise to live in, but He didn't do that either. He might have reminded them that He brought them into this world and that He could take them out if they didn't honor Him, but He chose to say something different.

What did our God say to them? "God blessed them; and God said to them, 'Be fruitful and multiply, and fill the earth, and subdue it; and rule over the fish of the sea and over the birds of the sky and over every living thing that moves on the earth.'"

"Be fruitful," He said! "Multiply…fill…subdue…rule…" These are the words our generous Father first spoke to those He had given life. Just as His first act reveals His heart, so do His first words to them.

The Joy of Creation

Don't think of this moment of creation as a solemn ceremony in which two people were inducted into the human race. This was the celebration heaven had anticipated. This was a defining moment in the dream the Father, Son, and Spirit had carried in His heart forever!

As you read this next part of the text, imagine the Creator breathlessly sharing this good news with His two just-brought-to-life children. Hear the pleasure in His voice.

> Then God said, "Behold, I have given you every plant yielding seed that is on the surface of all the earth, and every tree which has fruit yielding seed; it shall be food for you; and to every beast of the earth and to every bird of the sky and to every thing that moves on the earth which has life, I have given every green plant for food," and it was so (Genesis 1:29-30).

Can you hear the joy in the voice of Boundless Love as you read His words? "Look! Let Me show you what I have for you! Over here are the plants and trees that produce seed for all the great food you will need. And the animals—aren't they great? You'll rule over those. I've already made provision for their food too. I have it all taken care for you to enjoy—the animals, the birds…everything that moves is here for you to enjoy!"

Think about a time when you gave a special gift to somebody you particularly love. Can you remember the anticipation and excitement of sharing the gift with that person and of seeing the joy he or she would feel upon receiving the gift? Do you remember your joy at seeing that person's joy?

I remember celebrating my twenty-fifth wedding anniversary with my wife, Melanie. We married when I was 19 years old, so when I bought her engagement ring, I could afford only a small diamond. It might have been called a faith ring because it reflected "the assurance of things hoped for, the conviction of things not seen." We had both joked about it for years, and my intention had always been to buy her a more respectable ring when I was financially able.

As we approached our anniversary, I decided to make it a very special time. I planned a trip to Hawaii and told Melanie that this would be the way we would celebrate. What I didn't tell her was that I had also put a diamond ring on layaway at a local jewelry store. They kept the ring in stock, and I paid toward the cost each month. Just prior to our anniversary trip, the ring was paid off, and I brought it home.

When we went to Hawaii, I kept the ring hidden until the appropriate moment. We sat at the beach on Maui, under a waterfall…I was *so* excited about giving her the ring. I knew she would love it. I could barely contain my eager anticipation of seeing her response. The very thought of showing love to her in that way thrilled me.

That's your God. From the beginning, He delights in blessing you, in empowering you to live the life He created you to experience, and in giving you everything you need to fulfill the wonderful plan He designed for your life. He's no frugal, uptight, legalistic, cosmic killjoy. If you think of Him that way, you have Him confused with the god of dead religion. Our God is a joyful God, a dancing God, even a laughing God. He delights in seeing you happily receiving His love. The prophet Zephaniah gave the perfect description.

> The LORD your God is in your midst,
>   a mighty one who will save;
> he will rejoice over you with gladness;
>   he will quiet you by his love;
> he will exult over you with loud singing (Zephaniah 3:17 ESV).

Isaiah used a marriage metaphor. "As the bridegroom rejoices over the bride, so your God will rejoice over you" (Isaiah 62:5).

A New Picture of God

The beginning of the Bible gives us a picture of God that is very different from the image modern religion gives. When people form their opinion about God from what they hear from contemporary legalistic religion, it's no wonder they conclude that God is a cranky, old, book-keeping, judgmental, demanding deity who is more interested in people's behavior than anything else. It would be easy to see how a god like that would be angry much of the time.

Sadly, people who hold that view of God impose it on the Bible and interpret the Bible to present a God like that. Nothing could be further from the truth. I'm not saying that our God is a milquetoast, a mild-mannered god who can be managed. He's no kitten, that's for sure. C.S. Lewis addressed that in *The Lion, the Witch and the Wardrobe*.

> "Ooh!" said Susan, "I'd thought he was a man. Is he—quite safe? I shall feel rather nervous about meeting a lion."
> "That you will, dearie, and no mistake," said Mrs. Beaver. "If there's anyone who can appear before Aslan without their knees knocking, they're either braver than most or else silly."
> "Then he isn't safe?" said Lucy.
> "Safe?" said Mr. Beaver. "Don't you hear what Mrs. Beaver tells you? Who said anything about safe? 'Course he isn't safe. But he's good. He's the King, I tell you."[1]

No, our God is no domesticated deity that can be paper trained with a wrong understanding of Scriptures. But He's *good*. You can count on that.

The Two Choices

Into this garden of perfection God placed these two people. They had everything they needed to live in a blissful environment and a blissful relationship with their Creator. They were a mirror image of their God, living in a home designed by the One who makes rainbows and waterfalls and peacocks.

Then comes this statement about the Garden: "In the middle of the garden, God put the tree that gives life and also the tree that gives the knowledge of good and evil" (Genesis 2:9 NCV). These two trees in the center of the Garden would signal a fork in the road that would affect the destiny of mankind in ways Adam and Eve couldn't have even imagined. One was the tree of life, and the other was the tree of the knowledge of good and evil.

I have written extensively about these two trees in my first book, *Grace Walk*. I won't repeat that information here, but I do want to stress something about the tree of the knowledge of good and evil—its deadly nature.

Note carefully the name of this tree. It was a tree that gave knowledge, but knowledge of what? It gave knowledge of good and evil, of right and wrong. To eat from this tree would give Adam and Eve knowledge of what was right and what was wrong for themselves, knowledge they did not initially possess.

Moralism or Union?

Did Adam and Eve need to know good from evil? No, they didn't. This often-surprising fact creates a sharp dividing line between dead religion and authentic Christian faith. Religion is all about right and wrong. These two didn't need to know right from wrong for one simple reason—they lived every moment in the union they shared with their Creator. He was the source of their every thought, word, and deed. When they lived that way, their lifestyles were better than right. They were *righteous*.

The tree of the knowledge of good and evil was the tree that would introduce morality to the world. Notice that the tree had two aspects—good and evil. We might say that one branch bore good fruit and the other evil fruit. Human logic might lead us to believe that it would have made sense for God to tell them to eat from the good branch of the tree but never to eat from the evil branch.

That makes sense to most people today because we have been contaminated with a dualistic mindset that comes from the bitter fruit of that tree. This moral dualism focuses on good and evil. Humanity today is all about doing right and avoiding wrong, but that was not and is not the plan God has for you. He has a better plan based on your union with Him through Jesus Christ. The tree of the knowledge of good and evil can produce moral living, but only union with God can produce the lifestyle He intends for you—a miraculous life. Anybody can do right, but you're capable of living at a much higher level than morality.

Warning in Love

Here's the important thing about the tree of the knowledge of good and evil. To eat from it would be deadly. Take special note that disobeying God by eating from the tree would bring death. The loving Creator spoke to Adam and Eve and commanded them, "From any tree of the garden you may eat freely; but from the tree of the knowledge of good and evil you shall not eat, for in the day that you eat from it you will surely die" (Genesis 2:16-17).

Did He give this warning in anger? Of course not. The commandment not to eat from this tree was a tender expression of divine love. To eat from it would bring death to God's precious couple, so He told them in no uncertain terms that they must not eat from that tree, or they would die. It would certainly be fatal to them.

It's both amazing and sad to see how legalistic religion has butchered the meaning of this warning from a loving Father. If you have seen your God through the lens of legalistic religion, you most likely have believed that God was warning them that He would punish them if they ate from the tree. Nothing could be further from the heart or intent of God. *He* wouldn't kill them—*sin* would kill them. God wasn't warning them about what He would do but about what sin would do to them.

The first time the subject of sin is mentioned in the Bible, the point our God made clear is that sin brings death. Not God, but sin. File this away permanently in your mind because it will be the template that you will use as you read the rest of this book. More importantly, it will be the catalyst for change in the way you understand God. Look at the Genesis account again. God's heart was to protect, not punish. It was *sin* that would bring death, not Him. I've repeated this for emphasis. Lifelong mindsets don't instantly change, and this matter merits affirming the truth to yourself again and again until it becomes a foundational aspect of how you see God.

The Sour Note

Adam and Eve were dancing with Deity and loving every minute of it when suddenly the score to the drama shifted to a minor key. "Now the serpent was more crafty than any beast of the field which the LORD God had made" (Genesis 3:1). Do you hear it? Do you notice that with that biblical statement, the harmonious song of the dance between humanity and God seems to be interrupted with an off-key sound? For the first time in Scripture, a discordant note is heard on earth.

But there was no need to worry. The Great Dancer is also the Great Composer, and you will see how He fit the sour note into the overall majesty of the composition—His plan for us. Again, there's no duality in Him. Our God can synthesize the good, the bad, and the ugly into a beautiful masterpiece that leaves mankind standing in awe.

Take a look at the introduction of the serpent in the Garden of Eden. What is the first thing we learn about Satan in the Bible? He is crafty! He sometimes uses full frontal attack, but more often than not he takes a shrewd, sly, subtle approach to lead us away. Don't think it doesn't still happen. If Satan were writing his résumé, he would almost surely list many Christians' lives as some of the best demonstrations of his subtlety.

A Different Deity

Many have been deceived into embracing a faulty concept of who God is. In chapter 1 we saw that our God is a joyful, loving, generous Trinity who only loves and intends to share that love. In this chapter we step from heaven into time and see His loving nature once again as He interacts with man. No anger is seen here. Legalistic religion reframes the Genesis account and features a deity who becomes angered by the disobedience of those he created. The true God of the Bible is nothing like that.

That's why we should always be teachable when comparing our existing views with what the Bible actually says. We shouldn't be gullible, but each of us is wrong about some things, so how could any of us refuse to consider another viewpoint? Do we really think we have a perfect understanding of all biblical truth? We must submit our views to Scripture and to the Spirit as the final arbiters of truth. Never forget that you have a crafty enemy who wants to deceive you.

So this subtle serpent deceived Eve with a well-crafted lie. He introduced a false sense of inadequacy within her and what seemed like a noble desire to do something about it. "For God knows that in the day you eat from [the forbidden tree] your eyes will be opened, and you will be like God, knowing good and evil" (Genesis 3:5).

Be like God! Eve must have thought. *How could it not be a good move to do anything that would make me more like God?* That's the question people still ask today. The answer stems back to Satan's deception and Eve's misunderstanding. The fact is, she already *was* like God in every way that mattered. She was the mirror reflection of His image, but at the moment of temptation she felt insecure about that. Losing sight of her true identity and believing the lie that she needed to do something to become like God led to her downfall—and humanity's downfall ever since.

What had been God's assessment of all He had made? "God saw all that He had made, and behold, it was very good" (Genesis 1:31). That included Adam and Eve. In fact, it *especially* included them because they were made in His own image. But sadly, objective truth can lose its subjective influence in our lives when we allow ourselves to believe a lie. We can become blind to the truth and dead to the reality of who our Creator has made us to be. We can get lost in the darkness of unbelief and distrust.

Everything Changed

When you think of the word *sin*, what comes to mind? If you're like most people, you think about a moral infraction—lying, stealing, cheating, or evil things like that. But notice the subtle, crafty way Satan works. Eve committed the very first sin by trying to do something good. She wasn't trying to do wrong. She was trying to do right.

Eve disobeyed, but she surely must have rationalized that eating from the tree made good sense and that it was okay. In fact, she was so convinced that when she explained the whole situation to Adam, it made sense to him too, and he ate from the tree as well. One bite and then...

Instantly, everything changed. The music could no longer be heard.

The loving face Adam had so enjoyed seeing every evening suddenly appeared terrifying in his turbulent imagination. Everything now seemed dark. A condemning silence hung heavy in the air. The Garden of vibrant colors seemed to turn a stark, cold black and white. In an instant, Adam and Eve had become blind and deaf to all they had loved. In fact, it was worse than that. They *died*. They became the walking dead. Immediate physical death would have been a welcomed relief. The lengthening shadow of physical death fell across their now-deteriorating bodies, but that wasn't the worst of it. The immediate pitch-blackness of spiritual death was almost unbearable.

We Were There Too

Here's where the story gets even darker. Adam and Eve weren't the only ones who were affected by their disobedience. You were caught up in that cosmic mess too. All of humanity was there. *But I wasn't even born then*, you might protest. That's true, but you were there, in Adam, nonetheless. The fate of all mankind was bound up in him.

Think of it this way. Where would you be today if your grandfather or your father had died as a child? You wouldn't be here because your genetic origin was bound up in both of them. Whatever happened to them would have happened to you.

In the same way, the spiritual DNA of all humanity was tied to Adam. The result of his sin affected everybody who was to come. The Bible says, "When Adam sinned, sin entered the world. Adam's sin brought death, so death spread to everyone, for everyone sinned" (Romans 5:12 NLT). His actions didn't just affect him. They took us all down with him.

When David faced the mighty giant, Goliath, they weren't just two people meeting each other in a standoff. Israel and the Philistines were included in that battle. David and Goliath *were* those two nations when they fought each other that day. When David hurled the stone from his slingshot and it lodged in Goliath's forehead, causing him to fall straight to the ground, dead, that was the end. "When the Philistines saw that their champion was dead, they fled" (1 Samuel 17:51). They knew they had been defeated.

An important concept about Adam surfaces here, and it will help you much when we discuss the life of Jesus. It is the concept of vicariousness. When something is vicarious, it acts as a representative for something else. When Adam sinned, his vicarious act involved all humanity. When David killed Goliath, his vicarious victory affected every living Israelite and Philistine. The key thing to note here is that what one person does can affect everybody else.

What happened in the Garden of Eden wasn't an isolated incident. It affected the whole human race. Every person who would be born afterward was affected by that sin. Because of one man's sin, death reigned over every person (see Romans 5:17). The sour note of sin suddenly penetrated the beautiful melody of the eternal dance. The music played on, but on earth the tune fell silent, for Adam and Eve were now deaf to its melody.

The Consequences

In an instant, everything had changed. Spiritual light vanished from Adam's sight, and his mind was now engulfed in a darkness he had never known. For the very first time on planet earth, a human's thoughts frantically raced around, bouncing off newly constructed walls of anxiety and fear and worry and dread. It was hell. Darkness and an overwhelming sense of separation from Life Himself terrorized the two who comprised all of humanity at that moment.

Adam had lived for his sunset walks with God, but now, at the very thought of that time, his heart pounded with fear, and a palpable sensation of dread constricted his throat. What would the Creator say? What would He do? He had plainly commanded them not to eat from that tree. Hadn't God said they would die if they did? How would He kill them? Would it be swift and merciful? Would it be slow and agonizing? The very thought of facing God drove Adam and Eve to hide behind the bushes, afraid to see their Creator.

There it is. Look carefully at that scene. Study it. Think about it, because what happened in that moment may well still affect how you think about God right now. Adam believed that because he had done wrong, God would now relate to him as an angry judge. Before Adam and Eve sinned, they both saw God as the loving Father that He is, but from the moment they ate from the forbidden tree, their whole perspective of God changed. Since that moment, those blind to the truth still believe God is angered toward us by our wrongdoing.

Evening came.

> They heard the sound of the LORD God walking in the garden in the cool of the day, and the man and his wife hid themselves from the presence of the LORD God among the trees of the garden. Then the LORD God called to the man, and said to him, "Where are you?" (Genesis 3:8-9).

A person's tone of voice is everything in communication. At times it can communicate more than the actual words do. The way Adam heard the words "Where are you?" was completely different from the way God spoke them. You can be sure of that because Adam's perception of God had changed. The God of light and love now appeared dark and menacing.

The loving Creator asked the question with no malice, no anger, and no judgment. He may have meant, "Adam, do *you* know where you are?" Sadly, Adam didn't know. Reality had morphed into something ugly that bore no resemblance to what was true. What Adam heard was, "Okay, you unappreciative pile of dust! Where are you, and what have you done?"

Hiding from an Angry God

This scene illustrates a fundamental fact you must accept if you want to move beyond the image of an angry God and see your Father as He really is. Adam and Eve thought their sin would anger God and cause Him to punish them, so they hid in fear. What did God do? He came for His daily walk, just as He had always done.

God hadn't changed. Adam had. The fallout from what Adam and Eve did in the Garden of Eden still contaminates people's thinking about God today. They believe He knows about their sin and is angry about it and toward them. So they do exactly what Adam and Eve did— they try to hide. They duck behind momentary pleasures, behind the

acquisition of more and more possessions, behind the pursuit for pres-
tige. They even camouflage themselves with religious performance.
They wrongly imagine that God sees them through a judicial lens, as if
He were a hanging judge who is angry about their crimes, but nothing
could be further from the truth. That is *not* who your God is!

Punishment or Protection?

Once Adam and Eve acknowledged their sin, their Father outlined
the consequences to them. Sin brings consequences, but He would
be with them through it all. Some Bible readers think Adam and Eve
were driven out of the Garden of Eden as punishment from God for
what they had done. The Bible account reveals a different perspective.

> Then the LORD God said, "Behold, the man has become
> like one of Us, knowing good and evil; and now, *he might
> stretch out his hand, and take also from the tree of life, and
> eat, and live forever*"—therefore the LORD God sent him
> out from the garden of Eden, to cultivate the ground from
> which he was taken. So He drove the man out; and at the
> east of the garden of Eden He stationed the cherubim and
> the flaming sword which turned every direction to guard
> the way to the tree of life (Genesis 3:22-24).

Why did God drive them from the Garden? If He hadn't, they
might eat from the tree of life and live forever in the sad condition
they were in as a result of their sin. God drove them out of the Garden
of Eden for their own protection. Our God already had a redemptive
plan in mind, and He wasn't about to allow Adam to interfere with it.

That plan of redemption was foreshadowed before they were
expelled from the Garden for their own safety. "The LORD God made
garments of skin for Adam and his wife, and clothed them" (Genesis
3:21). God covered their nakedness with the skin of an animal. Later,
animals would be sacrificed in the temple to carry forward this foreshadowing of the One whose blood would take away the sins of the
world. In time to come, the perfect Sacrifice would appear, but here,
while the stench of their sin still hung heavy in the air, our Father

showed His heart of love and grace by covering them with the bloody skin of a slain animal.

Athanasius describes the heart of the Creator regarding Adam and Eve's plight.

> The thing that was happening was in truth both monstrous and unfitting. It would, of course, have been unthinkable that God should go back upon His word and that man, having transgressed, should not die; but it was equally monstrous that beings which once had shared the nature of the Word should perish and turn back again into non-existence through corruption. It was unworthy of the goodness of God that creatures made by Him should be brought to nothing through the deceit wrought upon man by the devil; and it was supremely unfitting that the work of God in mankind should disappear, either through their own negligence or through the deceit of evil spirits. As, then, the creatures whom He had created reasonable, like the Word, were in fact perishing, and such noble works were on the road to ruin, what then was God, being Good, to do? Was He to let corruption and death have their way with them? In that case, what was the use of having made them in the beginning? Surely it would have been better never to have been created at all than, having been created, to be neglected and perish; and, besides that, such indifference to the ruin of His own work before His very eyes would argue not goodness in God but limitation, and that far more than if He had never created men at all. It was impossible, therefore, that God should leave man to be carried off by corruption, because it would be unfitting and unworthy of Himself.[2]

That is who our God is. He will not stand idly by while those He loves are careening toward ruin. Though we make choices that would certainly deserve irrevocable consequence, our Father is a Father of Grace. Paul Tillich provides a more contemporary description of our situation and God's response.

Grace strikes us when we are in great pain and restlessness. It strikes us when we walk through the dark valley of a meaningless and empty life. It strikes us when we feel that our separation is deeper than usual, because we have violated another life, a life which we loved, or from which we were estranged. It strikes us when our disgust for our own being, our indifference, our weakness, our hostility, and our lack of direction and composure have become intolerable to us. It strikes when, year after year, the longed-for perfection of life does not appear, when the old compulsions reign within us as they have for decades, when despair destroys all joy and courage. Sometimes at that moment a wave of light breaks into our darkness, and it is as though a voice were saying: "You are accepted…" After such an experience we may not be better than before, and we may not believe more than before. But everything is transformed. In that moment, grace conquers sin, and reconciliation bridges the gulf of estrangement. And nothing is demanded of this experience, no religious or moral or intellectual supposition, nothing but acceptance.

In the light of this grace we perceive the power of grace in our relation to others and to ourselves. We experience the grace of being able to look frankly into the eyes of another, the miraculous grace of reunion of life with life. We experience the grace of understanding each other's words.[3]

Notice that God's act in covering them was of His own initiative. They didn't ask for that help. His decision to ban them from the Garden of Eden for their own protection was a mercy shown to them when they didn't even know they needed it. In fact, through the darkness of their own understanding, they probably left Eden wrongly believing that God was angry, that He was punishing them for wrongdoing.

A God Who Keeps Score

Perhaps the greatest ruin that came to mankind in the fall is man's distorted, perverted perception of God. Since that day, the religions of the world have built gods from the materials of their own shamed minds. Not knowing the truth of the God of Grace, they have created gods who are demanding in their expectations and quick to punish when those expectations are not met.

Sadly, this isn't only true of false religions. The same deadly misconception has usurped the lives of many who profess to be Christians. The problem is pervasive. Contemporary legalistic Christianity still imagines that God is keeping score based on our behavior. They see Him as a sort of divine accountant who is logging every failure and calculating the balance due.

> You would think, given the routinely low level of our performances at the higher reaches of our being, that we would, in our fantasies at least, welcome a respite from these inexorable audits—that we would imagine for ourselves romances in which the celestial bookkeeping department was given a long and well-deserved vacation. But no, we put it on overtime instead: however much we hate the *law*, we are more afraid of *grace*.[4]

Adam's sin in the Garden of Eden altered the way people would see God from that day forward. This was a great horror for mankind. As a result of Adam's sin, an open, vulnerable, transparent, and intimate relationship with God was replaced with fear, shame, guilt, and a sense of separation between the Creator and His beloved creation. People began to believe that God was a stern deity who watched them from a distance with a scrutinizing eye and an exacting sense of justice that demanded they be punished if they failed to meet His behavioral requirements.

Maybe you see God that way even now. If your understanding of who God is has been framed by the traditional teachings of a legalistic religious world, you're not likely to see Him in any other way. If you see your God as one who is primarily concerned about your actions, if you see Him as one who is disappointed when you do wrong, if you see Him as one who stands ready to punish those who fail and reward those who do their best to do the right thing, you have been taken captive by an Adamic view of God.

Changing Assumptions About God

Do you see the radical difference between the way Adam saw God before he sinned in the Garden of Eden and how he saw Him after he sinned? Which perspective more closely resembles the way you see Him? In your default setting, is He the Father who loves to walk with you, who wants to bless you and see you be fruitful? Or do you see Him as a judge who knows how you've behaved and isn't happy about it? Do you see Him as a Loving Father or more like a moral accountant who is keeping books on your thoughts, feelings, words, and deeds?

In a later chapter, you will learn how Jesus came into this world to reverse the damage done to humanity by Adam's sin. For now, will you acknowledge that perhaps you haven't seen your God through the eyes of Jesus but rather through the eyes of fallen Adam? From our consideration of what happened at the Fall, have you recognized some of your own faulty assumptions about God, similar to Adam's false assumptions?

This is vitally important because we can't possibly advance in our own grace walk beyond our concept of God. We will never move further into living in grace unless our concept of God's goodness grows. If you see Him as a cosmic critic who is watching and waiting for you to conform to what you imagine He expects from you, you will be trapped in feelings of spiritual inferiority and a misguided need for self-improvement. You will spend your life sewing coverings from religious leaves to make yourself look more presentable to God.

All this is unnecessary! The need for all mankind is to move away from the tree of the knowledge of good and evil and recognize that our identity doesn't come from Adam, but from Jesus Christ.

The events in the Garden may appear bleak, but we must not miss a statement in Genesis 3:15. Notice what God said to the serpent.

> And I will cause hostility between you and the woman,
> > and between your offspring and her offspring.
> He will strike your head,
> > and you will strike his heel (NLT).

Adam and Eve could take heart in these words. "There will be con-flict between you and the Descendant of this woman," God told him. "You will strike His heel, but He will strike your head." A blow to the heel is painful, but a blow to the head is fatal. "You will hurt Him, but He will destroy you," God told Satan. The hope of humanity rested in these words.

Chapter 3

Jesus Lived as Us

It was just the cry of a baby. Or was it? Something about it was like a faint tune on the radio in the background. You can't quite place it, but you know it's more than random sounds. The whimper of a little boy in a stall would have seemed mundane to most human ears, but to those who stood outside this box of space and time, it was the muffled cry of majesty.

Meanwhile, a few nondescript shepherds were standing out in a field making sure their sheep didn't wander off overnight. When heaven could bear it no longer, the clouds ripped apart, and from a portal connecting the seen with the unseen came a messenger—an "angel," to quote most translations. The shepherds immediately saw him and were scared out of their wits, "but the angel reassured them. 'Don't be afraid!' he said. 'I bring you good news that will bring great joy to all people. The Savior—yes, the Messiah, the Lord—has been born today in Bethlehem, the city of David!'" (Luke 2:10-11 NLT).

Then a whole choir of angels appeared around him, and in a

harmony nobody on earth was able to hear, they began to sing along
with the cry of the baby in the manger:

> Glory to God in the highest,
> and on earth peace, goodwill toward men! (verse 14 NKJV).

And thus it happened. The Music of Heaven had come to earth. He
had stepped down from ineffable beauty into an isolated barn outside
the city of Bethlehem. What God had promised Adam would happen
in the seed of the woman was finally coming to pass.

Love Incarnate

The church has long called this event the Incarnation. The word
doesn't simply refer to the birth of Jesus, but to His entire ministry as a
human being. Can you imagine that God the Son became human? It
staggers the mind to consider how great a love it would take to humble Himself to become one of us. He didn't simply look like a human.
He *became* a human being with all of the inherent physical weakness,
emotional vulnerability, and cognitive limitations that human beings
know so well. From the splendor of heaven into the brokenness of
humanity He came.

Athanasius wrote, "At one and the same time—this is the wonder—as Man He was living a human life, and as Word He was sustain-
ing the life of the universe, and as Son He was in constant union with
the Father."[1] Jesus didn't abandon His deity when He came into this
world. He continued living in the same union within the triune circle
that He had always enjoyed. The circle wasn't broken by His humanity.
Far from it—His becoming a man *enlarged* the circle so that mankind
would be included. He came to us to draw us in. Thomas F. Torrance
affirms this amazing truth.

> God is not some remote, unknowable Deity, a prisoner in
> his aloofness or shut up in his solitariness, but on the con-
> trary the God who will not be without us whom he has cre-
> ated for fellowship with himself, the God who is free to go
> outside of himself, to share in the life of his creatures and
> enable them to share in his own eternal Life and Love.[2]

God's choice to become a human being was an irrevocable pledge of divine love for the humanity He had created for that purpose. Torrance further affirms, "In Jesus Christ God has actualized his unconditional love for you in your human nature in such a once for all way, that he cannot go back upon it without undoing the Incarnation and the Cross and thereby denying himself."[3]

Jesus as the Last Adam

How did He actualize His love? It happened in ways that will thrill you beyond words when you clearly see them. His life was and is *your* life before the Father and is an expression of the Father's life to you. In a literal sense, Jesus was and is the divine mediator from both the Godward and human sides. He is God standing before humanity and humanity standing before God.

Jesus was the triune *Yes!* to Adam's temporal *no*. Just as everybody had been bound up in Adam, so we were united in Jesus. The Scriptures tell us, " 'The first man, Adam, became a living person.' But the last Adam—that is, Christ—is a life-giving Spirit" (1 Corinthians 15:45 NLT). The first Adam answered no to perfect dependence upon the Father, and as a result, sentenced humanity to death. The last Adam's perfect and eternal yes to the Father had the opposite effect on us.

This Man, the mediator of divine life, was a life-giving Spirit to us by virtue of His vicarious life. He didn't just do what He did *for* us; He did it *as* us. Jesus Christ took our entire human identity into Himself so that we would be able to take His identity into ourselves. The Son of God became a man so that mankind might become sons of God.

Jesus Lived for Us

The modern Evangelical world approaches the life of Jesus as if He were born for one reason—to die. That understanding falls far short of the richness of the Incarnation. Jesus didn't live in this world for more than three decades simply to pass time until He could be crucified. It wasn't simply His death that was vicarious on our behalf. His *life* in this world has great effect on us all as well. The implications of the vicarious life of Jesus touch every area of our lives, as Christian Kettler explains.

A vicarious sense of Christ's humanity signifies that Jesus Christ is both the representative of and the substitute for my humanity. He represents my humanity before God the Father, having taken my humanity upon himself, bringing it back to God from the depths of sin and death. He is High Priest, representing the people before God (the Epistle to the Hebrews). But he is also the sacrifice himself. He is the substitute, doing in my place, in my stead, what I am unable to do: live a life of perfect faithfulness to, obedience to, and trust in God. "Vicarious" at its heart means doing something for another in their stead, doing something that they are unable to do.[4]

The life of Jesus has vicarious application to our lives in important ways.

Vicarious Obedience

Consider the matter of obedience to God. Jesus was perfectly obedient to His Father. On the other hand, how often have we struggled to be obedient to the things we believe He expects of us? Here's a question worth seriously considering: What if obedience has nothing to do with conforming to demands on your external behavior? What if obedience, at its core, is simple faith in the complete obedience of Jesus?

Does this scenario suggest that our actions wouldn't matter? Of course not! To the contrary, it suggests that if it all revolves around the obedience of Jesus, we could abandon every self-effort to do the things we imagine God wants us to do and simply yield ourselves to the One whose record of obedience has already been given to us as a gift. Could obedience be as simple as relaxing from a religious struggle and trusting Him to be who He is and to live His life in our daily actions?

What if the issue of obedience had nothing to do with your willpower? The great news about Jesus's vicarious obedience *as you* before the Father is this: You don't have to struggle anymore. In fact, just the opposite—you can give up your struggle and simply rest in His finished work of obedience. The gospel of Jesus Christ isn't just good news for facing death. It's also good news for facing life!

The obedience of Jesus so far exceeds anything we could possibly do that it is absurd for any of us to struggle to be obedient. Trusting Him, not trying harder, is the pathway. Jesus was and is the Man who mediates your life to the Father. "And being found in human form, he humbled himself by becoming obedient to the point of death, even death on a cross" (Philippians 2:8 ESV). Jesus ascended the pinnacle of obedience through His death. What do we now foolishly believe we have to do? We have no trump card to play on the obedience of Jesus. We have the amazing offer to simply rest in what He has done.

The Heidelberg Catechism, written in 1563, affirms this.

> God, without any merit of mine, but only of mere grace, grants and imputes to me, the perfect satisfaction, righteousness and holiness of Christ; even so, as if I never had had, nor committed any sin: yea, *as if I had fully accomplished all that obedience which Christ has accomplished for me.*[5]

The obedience of Jesus Christ has been accomplished for you and given to you by grace. Just as Adam's disobedience was yours, Jesus's earthly life was *your* life of obedience to the Father.

It would be completely illogical for this dance of grace to be characterized by white-knuckled determination to do better. Our life is a divine dance, not some sort of disciplined duty that requires draining determination. What kind of dance would that be? The vicarious obedience of Christ frees you so that you can relax, listen to the melody of grace, and enjoy the dance, which is your life in Him.

Religion requires, but grace inspires. Jesus offers us an invitation.

> Are you tired? Worn out? Burned out on religion? Come to me. Get away with me and you'll recover your life. I'll show you how to take a real rest. Walk with me and work with me—watch how I do it. Learn the unforced rhythms of grace. I won't lay anything heavy or ill-fitting on you. Keep company with me and you'll learn to live freely and lightly (Matthew 11:28-30 MSG).

If your life is characterized by forced behavior that arises out of a sense of duty, you are missing the essence of grace in your lifestyle. It isn't supposed to be that way! Jesus calls you to "take a real rest." Does that mean we live in passivity and do nothing at all? It does not. Rather, it means we stop focusing on ourselves and scrutinizing the minutia of our every thought, word, and deed. Instead, we put our eyes on Jesus. Robert Capon masterfully explains this.

> The life of grace is not an effort on our part to achieve a goal we set ourselves. It is a continually renewed attempt simply to believe that someone else has done all the achieving that is needed and to live in relationship with that person, whether we achieve or not. If that doesn't seem like much to you, you're right: it isn't. And, as a matter of fact, the life of grace is even less than that. It's not even our life at all, but the life of that Someone Else rising like a tide in the ruins of our death.[6]

Obedience Is a Dance

I didn't grow up dancing. In fact, the message I received was that the reason premarital sex was wrong was because it might lead to dancing. Okay, maybe that's not true, but dancing was one of the big no-no's at my house. We could tap our feet to polkas and waltzes on *The Lawrence Welk Show*, and I could even sing along with the 1960s rock 'n' roll music of WRBN radio, but that's as far as it went.

My wife, Melanie, didn't grow up in such an environment. Lively music and dancing in the living room were as much a part of her family life as having meals together. Something about that caused me to envy her when we were teens. I wanted to dance, but I just didn't know how. Besides, I was afraid Jesus might come while I was dancing and was convinced that would be awkward.

Sometime around our twentieth wedding anniversary, we went on a cruise to celebrate. As we sat listening to the music and watching others on the dance floor, Melanie asked me, "Let's dance?"

"You know I don't know how to dance," I told her. I had taken her to two dances when we were in high school, but I stood on the sidelines and we didn't stay long. She didn't like it then and she still didn't like it.

"Come on, there's nothing to it," she responded. On the one hand I knew I didn't know how to dance, but on the other I wanted to please my wife. I sat silently for a few moments and watched the other men with their wives on the dance floor. I began to notice something I'd not previously known. Most men can't dance. They're just props for the women who do dance. I watched the guys shuffle back and forth from foot to foot with their arms bent and their hands raised to chest level and began to think that maybe I could do it after all.

"Okay, when they play a good song," I answered.

Shortly, the band began to play a song that caused Melanie to say, "Okay, let's go. This one is easy."

"What makes you think this is easy?" I asked.

"Because it's a cha-cha," she said. "Listen to the beat. It's one, two, one-two-three; one, two, one-two-three."

I took a deep sigh, and onto the dance floor we went. We started to dance. I watched my feet and consciously counted with each step: "One, two, one-two-three. One, two, one-two-three."

"Don't watch your feet," Melanie instructed. "This isn't hard."

"I can't talk to you and count at the same time," I replied as I lost count.

"Look at my face," she said. "Just relax and feel the rhythm."

I looked at Melanie's face and suddenly thought, *How did I end up married to such a beautiful woman—one who can dance?*

As the evening progressed, I found that what Melanie told me was true. When I relaxed and began to enjoy being with her instead of focusing on counting, I began to feel the rhythm of the music, and for the first time, I actually began to dance.

Before the week was over, I was dancing with my wife without giving a thought to my steps. I had forgotten all about how I was performing and was caught up in her. She was my focus.

Too many of us who are dancing become too preoccupied with making sure we don't miss a step. We're watching our feet instead of staring into the face of our Dance Partner. We're there, but we're not really *being* there. We need to relax, look at the One who brought us to the dance, and feel the rhythm of grace. It's not a matter of performing perfectly. The core of the matter is that your Dance Partner does dance perfectly, and He is leading you in this dance of grace called life.

The obedience of Jesus is yours to enjoy. When it comes right down to it, His obedience is the only obedience we *can* enjoy. We certainly don't have a track record that would allow us to rest on our own laurels.

As J. Gresham Machen, a great American Presbyterian theologian, lay dying, he sent this final telegram to his friend John Murray: "I'm so thankful for the active obedience of Christ. No hope without it."[7]

Don't focus on your performance and miss the peace that comes only by resting in His obedience. Trusting in Jesus's vicarious obedience gives us the freedom to live without self-scrutiny, without judgment of others, without trying to establish our own righteousness predicated on regimented religious rules. When we understand His active obedience, struggling becomes a moot point.

If you think I'm suggesting that obedience isn't important, I am not. Rather, I am asserting that the way of grace is to rest in His perfect obedience manifested in the circumstances of our lives. We trust Jesus to be Jesus in and through us from moment to moment. We don't try harder to do better, but we simply trust Him in every situation. Obedience to God lives in you, and His name is Jesus.

Vicarious Repentance

The subject of repentance has been wielded as a weapon against the naive for so long that the very mention of the word often conjures up harsh images of tearful remorse, heartfelt contempt, and the passionate dedication of oneself to God, laced with promises to "never do it again." The pseudo-repentance in much of the modern church focuses on sin, insisting that we single it out in our lives and, by the sheer force of contempt for it, eradicate it like a cancer. This religious "chemo" approach to sin might involve everything from bitter weeping to strict accountability to others about our behavior. Repentance is framed as a war against sinful thoughts, words, and deeds, drawing from the arsenal of sincere emotions and a ferocious will. Hit the sawdust trail and promise God you'll do better.

What if repentance doesn't have anything to do with emotional or mental upheavals accompanied by heartfelt commitments to change our evil ways? What if, like obedience, repentance is a gift we possess by virtue of the life of Jesus Christ? Could the coming of Jesus Christ into this world have *that* great an impact on mankind?

The biblical answer is a reverberating *yes!* Repentance isn't something we work up and use to get right with God. That has already happened for us through Jesus. Remember, He didn't just *die* for you. He *lived* on your behalf too.

A story in the Gospels bewildered me for many years. Matthew describes the scene.

> Jesus then appeared, arriving at the Jordan River from Galilee. He wanted John to baptize him. John objected, "I'm the one who needs to be baptized, not you!"
>
> But Jesus insisted. "Do it. God's work, putting things right all these centuries, is coming together right now in this baptism." So John did it (Matthew 3:13-15 MSG).

The apostle Paul called the baptism John performed a "baptism of repentance" (Acts 19:4). John's question was reasonable. In fact, it was the obvious question to ask. "Why do *You* need to repent?" John wanted to know.

The answer is, He didn't. Jesus wasn't baptized because He needed to repent. He was being baptized for you and me. The eternal plan was "coming together" when Jesus was baptized. The perfect Son of Man was acting for you just as surely as David acted for Israel when he faced Goliath. Jesus was doing "God's work, putting things right" in a way that John couldn't have possibly understood at the moment. You, on the other hand, can understand it now. His baptism of repentance was a *vicarious baptism.* Just as every other aspect of His life affects you, His baptism 2000 years ago has personal relevance to us all today.

Baxter Kruger stresses the significance of Jesus's actions.

The history of Jesus Christ is therefore not just another event in a series of important events in human history. The history of Jesus Christ is *the* event of all events. It is *the* moment of all moments. What happens here in this God, what happens here in this Son in and through and by whom all things exist, is of fundamental and decisive significance for you, me, the human race, and indeed the whole comos.[8]

This event, Jesus's baptism, certainly does have decisive significance for us all. Repentance isn't something we work up, but something that has been handed down to you as your birthright. Repentance is a gift, not a discipline. When Timothy was dealing with opponents, Paul wrote, "In meekness instructing those that oppose themselves; if God peradventure will *give them repentance* to the acknowledging of the truth" (2 Timothy 2:25 KJV).

When Peter preached the gospel to the Gentiles and many believed on Christ, some Jewish believers were upset by the inclusion of Gentiles. Peter explained in detail what had happened when he preached the gospel, and the others were finally convinced. "When they heard these things, they held their peace, and glorified God, saying, 'Then hath *God also to the Gentiles granted repentance* unto life'" (Acts 11:18 KJV).

God gives repentance to us through Jesus Christ. Does this mean that our thoughts and attitudes have no role in the matter of repentance? No, it doesn't. To truly repent, though, requires that we understand the meaning of the word.

The common understanding of repentance focuses on a person's decision to stop sinning and start behaving. That is not the correct meaning of repentance. The word actually denotes the act of changing one's mind. Does our behavior change when we repent? Of course it does. If our minds have been truly changed, how could our actions not follow? That, however, is the result of repentance, not the meaning of the word.

Why does this matter? It matters because when a person believes that repentance revolves around changing bad behavior into good behavior, his whole focus will be on behavior and not on Jesus Christ.

I've talked with many who have been mentally and emotionally tormented by the fear that maybe they didn't really repent enough when they believed on Christ. The truth is that we can relax about that matter. Repentance isn't hating sin strongly enough or changing your behavior drastically enough to be characterized as truly repentant.

To genuinely repent is simply to align our belief with the work of Jesus Christ. If you trust Him, there is nothing more you need to do. There's nothing more you *could* do because He has already done it all. Repentance is nothing more than changing our minds about Him and what He has already done to deal with sin. Do you want to be sure you have fully repented of all your sins? Then see them as having been decimated and taken away by His finished work. *That* is New Covenant repentance.

Repentance is joining our will to His work and resting in the fact that it is enough. It's not a mental exercise we struggle to do. Look at His baptism and align your will with His repentance on your behalf. Affirm that your trust is in nothing else but His finished work, and when you've done that, you can put to rest this idea about repentance as it relates to salvation. In that regard, you are done with repentance because "it is finished."

Repentance Is a Way of Life

On the other hand, there is a sense in which our life in Christ is a lifetime of repentance—of changing our minds as He leads us out of the old, faulty belief systems we have held and brings us into an ever-increasing knowledge of the truth, which can be known only in Him. Critics often argue that those who promote grace are soft on repentance, but nothing could be less true. To the contrary, we believe that as we grow in grace, our minds will continually be renewed to align with the truth. Deeply entrenched but erroneous views that have long held us captive will be uprooted by the One who will guide us into all truth (see John 16:13).

The critics of authentic grace are the ones who are soft on repentance. Legalistic religion makes us overly rigid. It causes us to believe we possess the single proper understanding of all things spiritual and have no further need to change our doctrinal perspectives. We forget that eternal truth is perfect but human understanding is not. We judge unfamiliar biblical viewpoints from our own paradigm and accept or reject them on the basis how they fit into our mental folders.

When we fall victim to legalistic religion, we often protest any understanding that contradicts our existing beliefs with the claim that any idea new to us isn't biblical. What we really mean is that a perspective that contradicts ours doesn't fit our present understanding of the Bible. We naively protest that any teaching we haven't already heard is a new teaching when in reality it is only new to us. We aren't open to anything that won't fit the self-designed template we use to evaluate everything.

That's why I assert that legalistic religion makes us soft on repentance. It makes us unwilling to repent. It keeps us from going to the Scriptures with an open mind and a prayerful attitude inclined toward understanding. When we are living in legalism, our knee-jerk reaction is to immediately dismiss anything that contradicts our existing views. With a ten-minute Google search and the validation of a few like-minded friends, our minds are made up about the matter.

Does this description sound harsh? I hope so, because much is at stake. It's altogether appropriate to gently awaken a person on a calm Saturday morning, but if the house is on fire in the middle of the night, more forceful measures are needed. Calls to repentance seldom sound gentle.

Some people charge that by emphasizing God's grace, we fail to teach repentance. That's ironic because legalism, not grace, prohibits us from repenting of our anemic, calcified view of the nature of our Father. As you read these chapters that focus on the Father's love and the centrality of Jesus's Incarnation, I hope you will ask the Holy Spirit to show you where you may need to change your own mind. Our eternal life is lived out in this human body, and faulty input from our cultural environment necessitates that we always be willing to repent of distorted views when we see them.

Vicarious Faith

Perhaps no aspect of our spiritual lives has been assaulted by legalism more than the area of faith. People have been made to feel inadequate, guilty, inferior, and hypocritical because of their supposedly weak faith. This is more common than attacks on just about any other issue related to Christian living. Ask average believers in typical churches how strong their faith is, and most will inwardly flinch because they feel as if they aren't doing very well in that area.

Many people see faith as a sort of currency we spend with God to get what we want or need from Him. The more of it you have, the bigger things you can buy. Many have blamed themselves for not having enough faith when things didn't turn out the way they had prayed and hoped they would. In one church, I was told that the pastor's wife had recently died because she didn't have enough faith to be healed. Others blame their lack of faith for unfulfilled desires about finances, relationships, career advances, family struggles, and countless other things. To these people, faith is something to be spent for gain, and if you don't have it, you lose.

To take such a viewpoint seriously leads the logical mind to ask, "How, then, am I supposed to have more faith?" To be told "Just have faith" sounds reasonable to the one saying it, but to the person hearing those words, it feels easier said than done. How are we supposed to wholeheartedly believe for something that we simply aren't sure is going to happen in our lives? Therein is the problem. It's a matter of misdirected focus. Allow me to illustrate.

I dabbled in sleight of hand tricks when my children were small. I was able to amuse them and sometimes even intrigue adult friends. As everybody knows, the key to most successful magic tricks is misdirection. Pretend to put something in one hand while you're really palming it in the other hand. Make people look up here when the action is really happening down there. Direct their attention toward what you want them to watch instead of what they would need to focus on to understand how the trick works.

This is exactly how people are tricked about the subject of faith. It's a matter of misdirection. Admonitions to have more faith usually direct our attention on two things—the level of our own faith and the outcome of the matter at hand. Do you notice anything important missing in this equation?

The missing element is Jesus! The challenge to have more faith about a specific outcome is often nothing more than a religious promotion for positive thinking. It becomes a matter of faith *in faith*. It is a subtle but effective use of misdirection. Nothing is wrong with positive thinking, but don't mistake it for faith.

People experience authentic faith when their focus is on the Faithful One. Faith is not wishful thinking enhanced by the steroids of positive expectations. Faith is confidence in the One who does all things well. Faith is the plain recognition of the presence of the One who determines and directs every outcome of every situation we will face in life. Faith is certainty based on the Person who is in charge of our circumstances regardless of the predicament we may be facing. In fact, our faith finds its very existence in that Person.

Many years ago, Melanie and I took sailing lessons. One day our instructor took us into a small cove, where he warned us that the winds were "squirrelly." As we sailed our small boat into the narrow bight, we began to feel as if we had been thrown into a clothes dryer. The wind seemed to come from every direction.

The sail was full when suddenly a gust slammed across our beam, and the boat heeled over toward the water. I watched in terror as the top of the mast almost touched the waves. Water flooded over the starboard railing, and I seriously thought we were going to sink. I didn't know what to do.

I glanced back at the instructor. He was standing on the stern with one foot on the inside and the other on the outside hull of the boat. He looked as calm as anybody I've seen. He had a slight smile on his face as if he were amused by our fear. For some reason, just seeing his expression calmed me. *He's the pro*, I thought. *If he isn't scared, I guess it's going to be okay.*

In a matter of seconds, the boat righted herself, and we were safe.

"You weren't scared at all, were you?" I asked him.

"No, I wasn't," he answered. "I knew the boat would turn up into the wind."

It's called "weather helm." I wish I'd understood the concept before going into that bight.

When we are facing the storms of life, we need to understand the importance of watching Jesus Christ. He inspires our faith, but even more, our faith originates from Him. He *is* our Faith. So then, faith isn't something we have to work up from within ourselves. Instead, it is Someone who lives within us who wants to work out every detail of life's journey. As we look at Him as our source of faith, we find a sense of that faith rising up within us.

Faith Is a Person

Just as obedience and repentance are ours through the indwelling Christ, so is faith ours to enjoy simply by recognizing that He is its source. Faith doesn't originate from us. The question is not whether your belief is big enough or strong enough or pure enough to receive the outcome you want. Faith is about Jesus! He doesn't hope for a certain outcome. He *knows*. You'll be much better off leaning into His faith than trying to crank out your own.

We depend on His faith because only His faith is perfect and never fails. Our trust is in Him because He is more than sufficient for every need we have and every obstacle we face in life. The faith you have isn't based on your ability to conjure up enough positive vibes to get the job done. It's not about us at all. "In Him we live and move and exist," Luke wrote in Acts 17:28. That environment of perfect faith is a good place to live.

Paul expressed the effects of understanding this reality in his own life: "I am crucified with Christ: nevertheless I live; yet not I, but Christ liveth in me: and the life which I now live in the flesh I live by the faith of the Son of God, who loved me, and gave himself for me" (Galatians 2:20 KJV). Note that he said that he lived his life by the faith *of* the Son of God. I cited the King James Version of the Bible here because the translators rendered that phrase correctly, something that not all translations do.

It is the faith *of* Christ that is ours. It is vicarious faith. He believes on our behalf, so all we need to do is trust Him. Just as I knew the boat wouldn't sink because of the obvious confidence of my instructor, I can trust in what Jesus knows to be true even when the external evidence points to a different conclusion.

We don't need to pray for faith. In Him we already have it. What we can muster up on our own isn't enough to move a grain of sand. If you doubt me on that, just try it.

In chapter 7 we will consider the distinction between faith *in* Christ and the faith *of* Christ, but for now take note that it isn't your job to manufacture faith. He (Faith) lives inside you and is more than able to rise to the occasion when faith is required, which is at every moment of life. Just as Jesus is your righteousness, peace, strength, and joy, so is He your faith. The union you share with Him is your only source for faith.

In moments when you feel as if your faith is weak, don't fall into the trap of trying to fake it until you make it. Just acknowledge your weakness to Him and lean into His certainty. When I looked at the face of my sailing instructor, I began to feel a sense of peace. I've found the same thing happens as I look to Jesus in the middle of a scary, menacing situation.

The apostle Paul understood this well. He knew that the greater issue is the faithfulness of God, not our own level of faith. Without mincing words he asked, "For what if some did not believe? Shall their unbelief make *the faith of God* without effect? God forbid: yea, let God be true, but every man a liar" (Romans 3:3-4 KJV). The basis of faith is God's faithfulness. He is faithful to do whatever He has said He will do. External evidence may suggest the contrary, but Paul counters, "Let God be true, but every man a liar."

Jesus Himself pointed to His Father's faithfulness as the foundation for faith. In Mark 11:22, He said, "Have faith in God." A literal translation would be, "Reckon on God's fidelity." Jesus reckons (counts) on the faithfulness of His Father. All we need to do is stand with Jesus on that.

The revelation of this truth will free you from trying to believe in your own strength. It will cause you to know that it isn't *your* faith that matters. In fact, there is no such thing as "my faith" because my faith is His faith, and His faith is based on His Father's faithfulness. The vicarious faith of Jesus Christ is your faith. What a relief!

Grace Gifts

Obedience, repentance, faith, and everything else we need to live the life we were created to live aren't virtues we produce and develop. They aren't even gifts we receive apart from Jesus. These qualities are already resident in us in this present moment because He lives in us, as Thomas Torrance explains.

> Grace is to be understood as the impartation not just of something from God but of God Himself. In Jesus Christ and in the Holy Spirit God freely gives to us in such a way that the Gift and the Giver are one and the same in the wholeness and indivisibility of His grace.[9]

All these gifts came to us from the Giver by Jesus and in His Spirit.

When that small baby cried out in Bethlehem, it was a cry of assurance to each of us that He was now here with us and that He would stand in for us before the Father on matters of obedience, repentance, faith, and every other aspect of our relationship to God. No wonder the angel called it "good news that will bring great joy to all people" (Luke 2:10 NLT). If ever an angel uttered an understatement, it was at that moment. The Incarnation of God in Jesus is the greatest moment that has ever occurred in time or eternity.

Chapter 4

Grace Isn't Fair

T hat's blasphemy!"

"No, it's not. You're just against me because there's no room in your hearts for what I'm teaching. This message will set you free if only you will take heed to it."

"We're already free and don't need you to tell us about God."

"Actually, you do. You're slaves and don't even know it."

"Well, at least we aren't bastards."

Ah, the deluded religious mind. Nothing is quite so calloused, confrontational, or cruel as a religious person whose sacred cows are being prodded with the stick of truth. When somebody's religious identity is being challenged, things are bound to turn nasty quickly. I was a local pastor for more than 20 years, and I love God's church, but I can tell you from experience, angry religious people can be terrible.

C.S. Lewis was right when he said, "Of all bad men religious bad men are the worst." Lest you become offended, let me assure you that the conversation above actually occurred between Jesus and the religious leaders of His day. It's found in John 8:31-43. Here's how The Message puts it.

> Then Jesus turned to the Jews who had claimed to believe in him. "If you stick with this, living out what I tell you, you are my disciples for sure. Then you will experience for yourselves the truth, and the truth will free you."
>
> Surprised, they said, "But we're descendants of Abraham. We've never been slaves to anyone. How can you say, 'The truth will free you'?"
>
> Jesus said, "I tell you most solemnly that anyone who chooses a life of sin is trapped in a dead-end life and is, in fact, a slave. A slave is a transient, who can't come and go at will. The Son, though, has an established position, the run of the house. So if the Son sets you free, you are free through and through. I know you are Abraham's descendants. But I also know that you are trying to kill me because my message hasn't yet penetrated your thick skulls. I'm talking about things I have seen while keeping company with the Father, and you just go on doing what you have heard from your father."
>
> They were indignant. "Our father is Abraham!"
>
> Jesus said, "If you were Abraham's children, you would have been doing the things Abraham did. And yet here you are trying to kill me, a man who has spoken to you the truth he got straight from God! Abraham never did that sort of thing. You persist in repeating the works of your father."
>
> They said, "We're not bastards. We have a legitimate father: the one and only God."
>
> "If God were your father," said Jesus, "you would love me, for I came from God and arrived here. I didn't come on my own. He sent me. Why can't you understand one word I say? Here's why: You can't handle it."

This kind of attack is all too common when somebody comes along portraying God the Father in a way that offends the pharisaical sensitivities of those whose lives are rooted in their religious dogmas and practices. Legalistic religionists can't get past the reality that God is not a judge who sits and scrutinizes our behavior. They think that God has placed divine expectations on us and that we had better make sure we meet those expectations—or else.

This particular conversation between Jesus and the religious powers that be was triggered when He demonstrated His love and tenderness to the woman caught in adultery. The crowd wanted to stone her. He wanted to save her. Pardon and payback have always been polar opposites.

The baseline of much religious conflict boils down to one issue—how loving is our God? Is He into payback or pardon or both? This may be the most important question you will ever answer because your viewpoint on this will affect everything. It will frame how you view God, others, and even yourself.

Harmonizing Justice with Love

"I believe God is a God of love but also a God of justice and even wrath," Leah said. "You can't leave those out without giving an unbalanced picture of the nature of God."

I perfectly understood her objection. There was a time when I would have given the exact same answer to any teaching about divine love that didn't make room for divine justice and wrath. Are justice and wrath aspects of God's nature, and if so, how do we reconcile them with the idea that God doesn't simply love but is *defined* by pure love at the very core of His essence? God doesn't just love. He *is* love. So how do justice, wrath, and love fit together?

In an attempt to affirm the love of God, some have rejected the concepts of justice and wrath altogether. But to reject something as plainly taught in the Bible as divine justice and wrath isn't a viable option for those who have a high regard for Scripture. Nor is it necessary to do so. Once we start dismissing biblical texts, where do we stop? No, we don't have to reject parts of the Bible to affirm divine love. Neither do we have to do interpretive juggling acts with these topics to avoid facing the fact that the Bible talks about them as aspects of our God's attitude and actions. Rather, we need to understand the words as they were used when they were written.

Theologian N.T. Wright said, "Just because some Western theologians cannot see how certain categories fit coherently together, doesn't mean that those categories didn't fit in the first century." That is the point we must remember when we try to understand biblical topics through our twenty-first-century mindsets. Some things don't mean what we may think they mean today. We need to take a closer look and allow the historical and contextual meaning of biblical passages and even individual words to speak for themselves. Randolph Richards and Brandon O'Brien explain this in their book *Misreading Scripture with Western Eyes*.

> To open the Word of God is to step into a strange world where things are very unlike our own. Most of us don't speak the languages. We don't know the geography or the customs or what behaviors are considered rude or polite. And yet we hardly notice. For many of us, the Bible is more familiar than any other book. We may have parts of it memorized. And because we believe that the Bible is God's Word to us, no matter where on the planet or when in history we read it, we tend to read Scripture in our own *when* and *where*, in a way that makes sense on our terms.[1]

Legal Justice

Consider the meaning of justice. The common contemporary understanding of the word *justice* can lead to a view of God that completely contradicts His true nature as revealed in Jesus Christ. This modern viewpoint finds its roots in the halls of jurisprudence and not in the heart of Jesus. It is solidly fixed in a system of law. It focuses on retribution, which balances the books by paying back those who have done wrong with a punishment that fits the crime. This approach to justice sees payback as morally correct and fully deserved. It guides the courtrooms of society.

This view of justice is the bedrock of American jurisprudence. Our Western idea of justice has its origins in sixth-century BC Athens with Solon, a statesman-poet-philosopher who lived in Greece during some revolutionary times. His goal was to transform the culture of retaliation that had marked society for hundreds of years.

Solon constructed the matrix for a democratic approach to justice through evolving constitutions that set a public court system in place, with juries of peers involved in an adversarial legal process and overseen by a presiding judge. The influence of this Athenian justice system can be seen in every courtroom in our land today.[2] It's the idea that when somebody does wrong, punishment is called for to make things right.

If you try to fit God into this template, you will see Him as a divine courtroom Judge whose sense of justice requires that He pass verdict and impose sentence on those who have done wrong. You will believe that consequences for sin are based on what is *fair*. In fact, fairness will govern your whole concept of divine justice. Viewing Him through this lens, it will be easy to imagine Him as an angry God.

You will read the Garden narrative in Genesis as if God punished Adam and Eve for what they did. Even worse, you will see the crucifixion of Jesus as punishment from God the Father instead of punishment from sin itself. You will see many tragic current events as expressions of divine anger and justice. From beginning to end, it will all be about a sort of justice that actually stands in tension with love. This stance acknowledges in principle that God is love, but it concludes that His hands are sometimes tied. He can express His love only in certain ways because His justice demands payback and He has to do what justice demands.

Restoration or Revenge?

Is there another way to look at this? There is, in fact, another understanding of justice, one that finds its roots in grace. It isn't concerned as much with retribution as it is with restoration. The goal in this expression of justice is to make the victim whole, to heal the offender and integrate him back into society as a productive person. Its aim is to make things right for everybody. It's not about payback. Instead, its purpose is to put back everything in the order it belongs. It's a biblical justice that finds its source in the very heart of our triune God.

Our God isn't an impartial judge or a dispassionate and distant governor. He is our *Abba* (Daddy), whose heart burns with love for those He has created. He longs to make things right in our lives so we can know and experience the life for which He created us.

Jesus didn't come simply to point out where we had created a problem. He came to fix it, and that's exactly what He did. He came to show us that while we may choose to live in the rejection Adam wrongly imagined when he sinned in the Garden of Eden, our God is into restoration, not rejection.

> If anyone hears what I am saying and doesn't take it seriously, I don't reject him. I didn't come to reject the world; I came to save the world. But you need to know that whoever puts me off, refusing to take in what I'm saying, is willfully choosing rejection. The Word, the Word-made-flesh that I have spoken and that I am, that Word and no other is the last word (John 12:47-50 MSG).

You can choose rejection, but Gracious Acceptance has chosen you and irrevocably embraced you. He has acted on His goodness, not our badness, and His goodness will forever be bigger than our badness. He has acted in justice to make things right for mankind because of the great love with which He has loved us. What we do with it is up to us, but what He has done isn't up for negotiation because "it is finished." You may choose rejection, but you don't get the last word. God is the great "I am," and "that Word and no other is the last word."

Justice that originates in the God of love is redemptive.

> God need not say, "I just can't get over my children's sin. I am so incensed with them. They are repulsive to me and trigger my wrath and need for vengeance. My hand is armed for their destruction. *Somebody* must pay me, and it has to be with punishment, with blood." But what if, alternatively, we imagine him saying, "I just can't get over my children. I'm so in love. I need to save them—even if it kills me."[3]

The heart of our triune God has always been one of restoration and reconciliation and not one of revenge. Consider this verse in Isaiah. As you read it, answer two questions: What does the Lord want to do for you? And why does He want to do that?

> Yet the LORD longs to be gracious to you;
>   therefore he will rise up to show you compassion.
> For the LORD is a God of justice.
>   Blessed are all who wait for him! (Isaiah 30:18 NIV).

What does God want to do? He wants to be gracious to you. He wants to show you compassion. Why? Because He is a God of justice! Does that sound like somebody who needs to balance the books by punishing you for what you've done wrong? This is the justice of agape, not anger.

How does this grace-based justice look in our relationships with other people?

- "This is what the LORD Almighty said: 'Administer true justice; show mercy and compassion to one another'" (Zechariah 7:9 NIV).

- "Learn to do right; seek justice. Defend the oppressed. Take up the cause of the fatherless; plead the case of the widow" (Isaiah 1:17 NIV).

- "This is what the LORD says to you, house of David: 'Administer justice every morning; rescue from the hand of his oppressor the one who has been robbed'" (Jeremiah 21:12 NIV).

Show mercy and compassion. Defend. Help. Rescue. These are words associated with justice that flows from divine love.

Jesus was sent to bring the Father's justice to humanity. What was that to look like? Here's the prophecy that described how He would bring justice into the world.

> Look well at my handpicked servant;
>   I love him so much, take such delight in him.
> I've placed my Spirit on him;

> he'll decree justice to the nations.
> But he won't yell, won't raise his voice;
>   there'll be no commotion in the streets.
> He won't walk over anyone's feelings,
>   won't push you into a corner.
> Before you know it, his justice will triumph;
>   the mere sound of his name will signal hope, even
> among far-off unbelievers (Matthew 12:18-21 MSG).

Have you ever seen God's justice in this way? You may have understood justice only through the template of retribution, but there is a higher way that expresses justice in grace. It's a way of restoration that lifts up and makes right the things that were wrong. Our Father is just to have forgiven our sin because Jesus righted the wrong done by Adam, and we all are the beneficiaries of His finished work.

Giving Up Fairness

The word *justice* is so strongly associated with revenge that it takes strong evidence and divine revelation of the truth for most people to change their minds about it. After all, it just wouldn't be fair if people got away with scandalous behavior without any punishment from God at all. At least that's what many think. I hope that by now you see that God's justice doesn't require Him to pay back those who have done wrong. Instead, in His justice, He has embraced us all and acted to restore us to the original image in which we were created—His image.

Here's the bottom line: Grace isn't fair. It's simply not. That may be why the apostle Paul said that grace is a scandal to the religious mind. He called it a stumbling block in 1 Corinthians 1:23, but the word in the original language of the New Testament is *scandalon*, from which we get the word *scandal*.

Robert Capon explains that nothing challenges our sanctimonious sensitivities like the idea of people getting away with something.

> In our fantasies, immorality can never be allowed simply to succeed; cosmic disapproval must be given the last word. The assignation is accomplished, but the lover's

water pump breaks down on the way home, necessitating a call to his wife to pick him up thirty miles off course. The beloved gives herself entirely, but her husband's firm moves him to Dallas, and out of the very givingness for which she is loved, she packs up dolls and dishes and goes sadly into the sunset. Or she loses a child in a fire that starts while she is in the motel with her lover. Or her lover loses his nerve. Or they marry at terrible cost and both lose their interest. Whatever happens, the books are always balanced, the notes due called in, the mortgages foreclosed.[4]

Moralism

That description is based on an expectation that came directly from the tree of the knowledge of good and evil. Only when Adam ate from that tree did morality and immorality become the framework on which lifestyles are built and the criteria by which they are judged. Until then, no such moral dualism existed. Everything was God, and that was enough. The lingering lie from Eden still hangs heavy in the suffocating air of moralism. Not just morality, but moralism. It has become the prevailing religion of the world, and modern Evangelicalism has not escaped its contaminating influence. Moralism exalts good morals as the principle aspirations of a life well lived. It advocates the age-old lie that sooner or later, we all get what we deserve. It may be good. It may be bad. That all depends on how we behave now.

Jesus's ministry is a stark denial of this lie. His whole life was a testament to a grace that transcends moral fairness. That is precisely the reason He infuriated the religious moralists of His day. His message of grace still does. Jesus showed the sharp distinction between grace and human fairness in no uncertain terms.

> For the Kingdom of Heaven is like the landowner who went out early one morning to hire workers for his vineyard. He agreed to pay the normal daily wage and sent them out to work.
>
> At nine o'clock in the morning he was passing through the marketplace and saw some people standing around doing

nothing. So he hired them, telling them he would pay them whatever was right at the end of the day. So they went to work in the vineyard. At noon and again at three o'clock he did the same thing.

At five o'clock that afternoon he was in town again and saw some more people standing around. He asked them, "Why haven't you been working today?"

They replied, "Because no one hired us."

The landowner told them, "Then go out and join the others in my vineyard."

That evening he told the foreman to call the workers in and pay them, beginning with the last workers first. When those hired at five o'clock were paid, each received a full day's wage. When those hired first came to get their pay, they assumed they would receive more. But they, too, were paid a day's wage. When they received their pay, they protested to the owner, "Those people worked only one hour, and yet you've paid them just as much as you paid us who worked all day in the scorching heat."

He answered one of them, "Friend, I haven't been unfair! Didn't you agree to work all day for the usual wage? Take your money and go. I wanted to pay this last worker the same as you. Is it against the law for me to do what I want with my money? Should you be jealous because I am kind to others?" (Matthew 20:1-15 NLT).

The obvious point of this parable provokes outrage from religionists obsessed with fairness. The insistence on fairness is really an admission of our own self-righteousness. Do we really want what's *fair*? Let him who is without sin cast the first vote for fairness.

Do You *Really* Want What's Fair?

Jesus often said things like this. His words revealed the hidden arrogance that so often crouches beneath the polished performance of religious fervor. Until we are set free from legalistic notions of fairness, we think that good behavior should somehow gain God's nod of approval and bad behavior should produce punitive results from Him. But that's just not how it works. Grace is indiscriminate, and what matters is belief and acceptance, not a good day's work for a good day's pay. Grace is a gift, not a paycheck.

Robert Capon does a masterful job explaining the scandal of pure grace that ignores the classic construct of fairness. In his typical style, which sometimes offends squeaky-clean religious sensitivities, he offers his take on Jesus's response to the workers who insisted on fairness instead of grace.

> "Look, Pal," he says. (Incidentally, the Greek word in the parable is *hetaire*, which is a distinctly unfriendly word for "friend." In three of its four uses in the New Testament— here, and to the man without the wedding garment in the King's Son's Wedding, and to Judas at the betrayal—it comes off sounding approximately like "Buster.") "Look, Pal," he tells the spokesman for all the bookkeepers who have gagged on this parable for two thousand years, "don't give me *agita*. You agreed to $120 a day, I gave you $120 a day. Take it and get out of here before I call the cops. If I want to give some pot-head in Gucci loafers the same pay as you, so what? You're telling me I can't do what I want with my own money? I'm supposed to be a stinker because you got your nose out of joint? All I did was have a fun idea. I decided to put the last first and the first last to show you there are no insiders or outsiders here: when I'm happy, everybody's happy, no matter what they did or didn't do. I'm not asking you to like me, Buster; I'm telling you to enjoy me. If you want to mope, that's your business. But since the only thing it'll get you is a lousy disposition, why don't you just shut up and go into the tasting room and have yourself a free glass of Chardonnay? The choice is up to you, Friend: drink up, or get out; compliments of the house, or go to hell. Take your pick."[5]

When Jesus told this parable, it had the same effect on people that Capon's retelling of the story has on some today. How can He draw

such a sharp line in the sand and vehemently insist with such an offend-
ing certitude that it has to be either all grace or no grace? Can't it be,
"Well, yeah, we're under grace *but...*"? No, it cannot. Any qualifying
requirement for grace destroys grace. As Capon so bluntly asserted, it's
either drink up or shut up. We are under grace—period.

Prodigals and Pious Sons

Perhaps the most well-known illustration of the way grace transcends fairness is the parable of the prodigal son in Luke 15. Here is a
young man who insists on having his inheritance while his father is still
alive, takes it to a distant city, and foolishly spends every penny of it on
self-indulgent gratification. When the money runs out and he finds
himself alone, broke, and hungry, he has to come up with a plan. Jesus
described the boy's attitude when he finally found himself in dire straits.

> He would have gladly filled his stomach with the pods that
> the swine were eating, and no one was giving anything
> to him. But when he came to his senses, he said, "How
> many of my father's hired men have more than enough
> bread, but I am dying here with hunger! I will get up and
> go to my father, and will say to him, 'Father, I have sinned
> against heaven, and in your sight; I am no longer worthy
> to be called your son; make me as one of your hired men'"
> (Luke 15:16-19).

The son doesn't have an ounce of regret about the way he had
insulted his father by asking for the inheritance before he died. He
shows no concern about his father's feelings. He doesn't exhibit one
pang of conscience about how he had spent the money. This young
prodigal's actions and words show that he is completely self-absorbed.
As far as we can tell from the text, he goes home just to get a meal and
a warm bed. That's all.

When his father sees him on the horizon, he runs out to meet him,
beside himself with joy. With open arms he falls on him, hugging and
kissing him. The son, on the other hand, has an agenda. He needs to
secure a home and has already made his plan.

He attempts to give the speech that he had probably rehearsed all the way home. "Father, I have sinned against heaven and in your sight; I am no longer worthy to be called your son." He had planned to apply for a job as a servant, but he never got that far into his spiel. His father interrupted him, calling out to the servants.

> Quickly bring out the best robe and put it on him, and put a ring on his hand and sandals on his feet; and bring the fattened calf, kill it, and let us eat and celebrate; for this son of mine was dead and has come to life again; he was lost and has been found (verses 22-24).

For many years I believed and taught that the prodigal repented when he arose from the pigpen and came home, but I was wrong. He didn't repent then. He only had a new plan for moving ahead. He was like the person who rededicates himself to God, promising to avoid sin and work hard for Him if He will just forgive him. It's religious nonsense. Our Father doesn't want that any more than the prodigal's father did. What He wants is *us*. He wants us to relax and simply enjoy our relationship to Him. Grace cannot connect with the one who promises to try harder. The nature of grace makes that impossible. It can connect only with those who have given up.

Your Side of the Bargain

This sort of relaxed approach to God doesn't sit well with many of us. Our concept of fairness leads to the foolish notion that we must offer something to make the transaction work. Rededication and efforts at rehabilitation are idolatrous attempts to make a contribution of some sort. In reality, we need to realize that we have nothing to contribute and need nothing to contribute. If there is a transaction, it's one-sided. God has already done it all on our behalf, and the only thing left for us to do is believe it really is finished.

> Creation is not ultimately about religion, or spirituality, or morality, or reconciliation, or any other solemn subject; it's about God having a good time and just itching to share it.

The solemn subjects—all the weird little bells, whistles, and exploding snappers we pay so much attention to—are there only because we are a bunch of dummies who have to be startled into having a good time. If ever once we woke up to the fact that God finally cares about the party, then the solemn subjects would creep away like pussycats ("Thank God! I thought they'd never leave!") and truly serious subjects would be brought on: robes, rings, shoes, wines, gold, crystal, and precious stones.[6]

Fairness balks and asserts that divine justice won't allow it to be that easy, but it is. This is a point where, like the prodigal, we may need to repent. This kind of repentance is needed across the board in the church world today. Our sense of fairness must give way to faith in the outrageous goodness of our heavenly Father. Until we see ourselves as dead in our self-effort, we will remain there. We don't need to do anything, but only need to own our deadness. There can be no resurrection apart from death. We must repent of the idea that it's only fair that we promise God to try harder. Repentance isn't about changing our behavior. It's about changing our minds and the way we see God. That's the only thing that can lead to further change.

> So the spiritual Way proves to be a path of repentance in the most radical sense. *Metanoia*, the Greek work for repentance, means literally "change of mind." In approaching God, we are to change our mind, stripping ourselves of all our habitual ways of thinking. We are to be converted not only in our will but in our intellect.[7]

But What If...

There you have it—the unfairness of grace. The prodigal shows up, the father tears up, the barbeque fires up, the music starts up...and out walks the older brother. It's no wonder he storms out of the house irked and sulky. We can talk all we want about how self-righteous he was, and technically, we wouldn't be wrong. But let's be honest. Anybody with the slightest sense of fairness would have felt the same way. Some things just aren't fair!

That's the point. Fairness suffocates for lack of oxygen in the grace-saturated environment of unconditional love. "Fair?" the father might have asked. "Are you nuts? This is *my son*, and he has come home!"

The older brother still lives today. Holding a stellar résumé of impeccable ethics and flawless service, he is totally put off by the idea that our Father's grace is that sloppy. Embrace a pig-manure-covered rebel whose sole motivation for coming home is to reap yet something *else* for himself? It's ludicrous! Where's the sense in that? What does it say to that misbehaving son? What wrong impressions will others get about the Father when they see such indiscriminate acceptance? What misunderstanding does it communicate about the importance of right behavior? What kind of wrong ideas will it cause other people to get about sin? How is that fair to all those who give their lives to doing right?

The avalanche of objections will continue from this older brother, but it won't change the Father in the slightest. He knows what He is doing and isn't affected in the least by our distorted sense of injustice. He just patiently smiles when we roll our religious eyes about the wrongness of it all. In these moments, when we see glaring and garish grace, we witness the nucleus of our God's heart and the reason for our own existence. That reason is to be known and to be loved. Perhaps you will never see a more sacred moment of grace than when filth is absorbed into and absolved by unconditional acceptance.

Such grace throws our sense of fairness into convulsions. But in these observations of raw grace, we see the essence of the relationship between the Creator and the created. Kallistos Katafygiotis rightly noted in the fourteenth century, "The most important thing that happens between God and the human soul is to love and be loved."[8] That is the meaning of life in nutshell.

Did Jesus Really Reveal the Father?

"But what about all those verses in the Old Testament that show God as being angry and bringing judgment on people?" Kip asked me one day after I had taught about justice from the nonpunitive perspective of the New Covenant.

"There's no doubt that verses in the Old Testament do speak in a way that could cause us to believe that God the Father stands ready to pay back evil with evil, but in light of the New Testament revelation of our Father as revealed to us in Jesus, might there not be another way to understand this matter?" I asked him.

"How would that look?" he asked.

It was a good question. The writer of Hebrews demonstrates an important principle in understanding the Bible. Some have called it the Christological principle, meaning that when we interpret the Scriptures, we must see every text through the lens of Jesus. He is the final Word on the Father. Let's look again at Hebrews 1:1-3.

> God, after He spoke long ago to the fathers in the prophets in many portions and in many ways, in these last days has spoken to us in His Son, whom He appointed heir of all things, through whom also He made the world. And He is the radiance of His glory and the exact representation of His nature, and upholds all things by the word of His power.

People who view God the Father through a judicial lens and thus see Him to be a divine courtroom Judge are drawn like a magnet to Old Testament verses about God's justice and wrath. To be sure, some verses are difficult to understand in light of the New Covenant teachings about the love of God. But to understand these Old Testament passages, which are difficult to reconcile with the Father as Jesus revealed Him, how should we proceed? Should we build a theology around them? Or might it make more sense to interpret the Old Covenant texts in light of the New Covenant revelation brought to us in Jesus?

Did Jesus successfully and effectively reveal His Father to us? Old Testament saints got glances of the Father, but in Jesus Christ, New Covenant believers are able to gaze into His heart. As the writer of Hebrews says, "He is the *radiance* of [the Father's] glory and the exact representation of His nature."

The English word *radiance* literally means "out-raying," just as sun-beams are expressions of the sun itself. Did Jesus reveal the Father to us or not? If He really did "out-ray" the Father, where did He show us an angry side that motivated Him to bring retribution on people?

A God like Jesus

Does Divine Love, who led Paul to write that love "is not provoked, does not take into account a wrong suffered," now do those very things? Did Jesus tell us to forgive those who hurt us and not repay evil with evil, knowing full well that His Father stands poised to do just the opposite? Did God place demands on us that even He won't keep? Did Jesus leave out half the story, not telling us about the dark side of His Father, but only telling us a part of the story by showing His good, gracious side? No, most assuredly not.

It is time for serious lovers of God and students of the Bible to rethink some things we have been told. Yes, some texts are hard to harmonize with what we know about our Father, but let us not smear the character of Pure Agape with slanderous assertions that contradict everything Jesus showed us about His Father because of our inability to understand.

What are the answers for those Old Testament texts? Numerous answers may apply, depending on the passage. Sometimes a verse that seems to stand in contradiction to the loving nature of God can be properly understood if we take the time to study it. Other verses seem to lead us to a roadblock when reconciling them with Jesus's revelation of the Father.

Charles Hodge was a renowned nineteenth-century theologian who argued strongly for the authority of the Bible as the Word of God. Fundamentalists and Evangelicals adopted many of his ideas in the twentieth century. What did this theologically conservative, Bible-believing scholar say about these troublesome texts?

> The progressive character of divine revelation is recognized in relation to all the great doctrines of the Bible. What at first is only obscurely intimated is gradually unfolded in subsequent parts of the sacred volume, until the truth is revealed in its fullness.[9]

Plainly put, don't expect to find as much understanding from the Old Testament as you do from the New Testament. This in no way minimizes the value of Old Testament passages. Rather, it points toward a proper framework for understanding the Scriptures. That is especially important when considering difficult issues like the one we are addressing.

Augustine, one of the Church Fathers, also commented on the relationship between the Old Testament and the New Testament when he said, "In the Old Testament the New Testament is concealed; in the New Testament the Old Testament is revealed." As Scripture unfolded and the people of God moved forward, they experienced a progressive and increasing understanding of truth. So we put ourselves in a dangerous place when we formulate concrete opinions about who God is without filtering our thoughts through Jesus. The Old Testament is certainly inspired Scripture, but it must be understood in light of the New Testament revelation through Jesus Christ.

To have a healthy and proper understanding of God, we must move beyond the idea that He is an angry, punitive magistrate who is more preoccupied with balancing the books than He is with us. Your Father is *for* you, and Jesus came to reveal that. There is no side to God the Father that looks different from the compassionate grace demonstrated by God the Son.

Chapter 5

Jesus Wasn't Forsaken

God turned his back on Jesus so He wouldn't have to forsake us. The Bible plainly says that," a pastor said to me at lunch one day. "Some things are clearly taught in the Bible and shouldn't be denied. Your teaching denies God's justi... t's not biblical!"

His concern about my t... ing isn't uncommon. Many believe that Jesus's death satisfied the F... by balancing the books so that we now don't have to be recipient... ine justice and wrath. Having read the previous chapter, how ... ou have answered this man's concern about divine justice be... ed?

I knew this pastor ... felt free to respond to him directly. "Jim, I think your accusati... esumptuous. You know me. You know I haven't come to my ... standing about this without a lot of Bible study and prayer—j... n fact. If you want to insist that this isn't the way *you* understand ... nterpret the Bible, that's okay. But don't tell me it isn't biblical j... ecause it's not the way you see it right now. If you're open to it, I'd ... more than happy to take some time and show you from the Bible what led me to this understanding."

Sadly, it didn't work out that way with Jim. He had made up his mind and wasn't interested in hearing the biblical evidence that has led countless Christians throughout church history to see the work of Christ on the cross in a way that is different from what many of us have been taught.

How Did the Atonement Work?

The traditional approach has left many with a concept of God the Father that makes it practically impossible not to see Him as an angry God. This teaching has four main points.

1. God is a God of justice and must act fairly in every matter.

2. Humanity has sinned and must be punished. Otherwise, God wouldn't be just.

3. Jesus loved us so much that He took our place on the cross, and God the Father poured out His anger on Jesus so He wouldn't have to punish us.

4. As a result, God the Father will forgive us for our sin if we will simply ask and trust Him to.

This is probably the teaching most of us have received about the atonement of Jesus Christ on the cross. It is the predominant viewpoint in the Western world. This view is called the penal substitution theory of the atonement. The word *penal* indicates that the crucifixion was punishment by God the Father. *Substitutionary* points to the fact that Jesus took our place on the cross. This is the only way many have been taught about the cross, so they assume it's the only way to understand Jesus's crucifixion. Actually, that's not the case at all.

Believers through the years have understood the crucifixion of Jesus in several ways. None of them deny the Scripture. They are simply different ways of interpreting it. The penal substitution theory I have outlined above is just one of them. Others include the ransom theory, the recapitulation theory, the moral influence theory, the satisfaction theory, and the *Christus victor* theory. Some of these theories are very similar, such as the penal substitution theory and the satisfaction theory, or the *Christus victor* theory and the ransom theory. Some are very different from the others.

Although the penal substitution theory is the most popular in Evangelical churches, a large part of the Christian world has *never* understood the atonement that way. Since New Testament times, these believers have had a different interpretation of what happened when Jesus took our place on the cross. Their understanding has nothing to do with God the Father forsaking His Son there and punishing Him in our place. Yes, Jesus did take our place—that part is correct. He was punished. That's true too, but *not by His Father*. More about that later.

Augustine's Influence

First, it is important to recognize how easy it is to think that there is only one way to understand a matter. If we have only heard one point of view on something, we are unlikely to question it. In fact, it doesn't even occur to us that it *could* be questioned. When somebody does question the prevailing viewpoint, there is often a knee-jerk reaction from people like Pastor Jim because the one questioning seems to be treading on sacred ground and denying something that everybody supposedly knows is true. We must rise above this cultural blindness in order to grow in grace.

Two leaders who had tremendous influence in the early church left an imprint that still impacts us today. The Western church leaned toward Augustine's interpretation of the atonement, and the Eastern church emphasized Athanasius's teaching. Both men were important in guiding the understanding that Christians have today. Both made positive contributions to the development of Christian thought, but they didn't approach some things the same way.

Augustine lived during the late fourth and early fifth century. You have probably heard of him but may not know that some of the things you believe are almost certainly the direct result of his teachings. They still have great influence on much of the church.

The Influence of Culture

You may protest that your beliefs come from what the Bible plainly says and have nothing to do with what somebody else said or wrote. The problem with that kind of denial is that nobody reads the Bible in a vacuum. In other words, your *method* for understanding what the Bible says has been guided by your culture and by those who have helped shape it. It isn't a question of what the Bible says. That isn't the issue. The question is, what does the Bible *mean* by what it says? We can all agree on what it says. All that takes is literacy. But when we begin explaining what it means, we don't always agree.

Church history is a 2000-year discussion about what the Scriptures mean regarding one thing or another. If you think that everything you believe is the obvious truth and that any other way of seeing it is wrong, remember that your beliefs are shaped by cultural factors—where you live, when you live, the church you attend, where you were educated, and other factors. To ignore these influences is to be blind to the power of the culture.

We aren't usually aware of this blindness. We don't know what we don't know. Bible students who approach the Bible with a high level of scholarly integrity, a high view of Scripture, and sincere trust that the Holy Spirit will guide them often come to different conclusions about what the Bible means about various topics.

Why can't we all agree? That's the question many have asked. The answer is simple—we are finite beings seeking to grasp eternal truth. Our finite minds are capable of receiving revelation of biblical truth from the Holy Spirit, but as the apostle Paul wrote, "We have this treasure in jars of clay to show that this all-surpassing power is from God and not from us" (2 Corinthians 4:7 NIV). In other words, we live in human bodies and don't have perfect understanding of everything. That's why it's important to hold our views in humility and to recognize and respect other people's beliefs.

Some people say, "Well, the Holy Spirit taught me!" It's true that the Holy Spirit is our Teacher, but what are you going to do when other people say the Holy Spirit taught them something very different from what you believe? That is where humility and respect need to rule the situation. The Holy Spirit never tells anybody something wrong. His broadcast signal is always perfect, but our reception is sometimes not so perfect.

The Bible certainly isn't the problem. All Scripture is given by inspiration by God. The snag is in our human understanding. Believers have wrestled with some of these matters for centuries. If we think we have a perfect track record in coming to objective, factual, from-His-mouth-to-my-understanding interpretations of biblical truth, we have made a serious mistake. Of course, we can know things, but when we insist that our viewpoint about a matter that has been debated for centuries is *the* definitive answer, we are...well, there's no other word for it—we're arrogant.

> There is no purely objective biblical interpretation. This is not postmodern relativism. We believe truth is truth. But there's no way around the fact that our cultural and historical contexts supply us with habits of mind that lead us to read the Bible differently than Christians in other cultural and historical contexts.[1]

Athanasius's Perspective

Eastern Christianity provides a cultural and historical context that is different from ours and that doesn't embrace the penal substitution theory. The primary influence in these churches was Athanasius.

An Augustinian approach to sharing the gospel usually begins with the problem of sin, and then it progresses toward the solution in the cross. Many soul winners learned to start with Romans 3:23 when sharing the gospel—"All have sinned and fall short of the glory of God." That is a decidedly Augustinian approach to evangelism. Athanasius came at it from a different direction. His tack started with the love of our triune God for those He created, and then it moves toward humanity's need. It is based on the Trinity's loving intention to embrace mankind and include us in the divine circle of love and life.

Is God on Our Side?

When we start with the understanding that *God is love*, we see the cross in a new light. Consider the common view of the crucifixion. Did God the Father pour out His anger on Jesus so we could be spared? Did He abandon His Son on Calvary? If so, was there a schism in the

Godhead at that moment, with the Son showing compassion and love toward us while His Father was pouring out onto Jesus the rage that our sin caused Him to feel toward us?

In this scenario, the Son would clearly be on our side, but what about the Father? If He had to vent His anger about our sin onto Jesus so that He could be okay with us, what does that say about Him? Why didn't Jesus feel that same anger? In that scenario, one might wonder if the Father loved us as much as Jesus did. God the Father was supposedly angry and had to express His wrath to satisfy His "justice." But Jesus wasn't angry toward us. In fact, He was willing to accept the Father's anger so we could avoid it. That's a strange interpretation, but it is widely accepted as true. No wonder many Evangelical Christians feel close to Jesus but not to His Father!

Is this really a good-cop, bad-cop situation? God the Father found it necessary to administer severe punishment on us, but God the Son found a legal loophole that allowed us to be spared. Is that what "justice" demanded? Unless God the Father is nothing like His Son, that makes no sense whatsoever.

In reality, the Father, Son, and Holy Spirit were *all* involved in rescuing us from sin's penalty.

You can be assured that your Father has *never* felt differently toward you than the Son does. The Father, Son, and Holy Ghost have forever loved you. God the Father was in Christ, says the apostle Paul, "reconciling the world to Himself." Where was the Spirit in all this? Hebrews 9:14 says that Jesus offered Himself through the eternal Spirit. The Spirit empowered Jesus, the Son of Man, to do what He did.

The idea that the Father stood apart from the Son while Jesus died for our sin has long been a misunderstanding among many Christians. Tell some people that the Father didn't abandon Jesus at the cross, that He was actually a loving, active participant in the work of Calvary, and you'd better be prepared for a debate.

"What do you mean, 'The Father didn't forsake Jesus on the cross?'" Carlos asked. "Jesus Himself said the Father forsook Him."

"When did Jesus say that, Carlos?" I asked him.

"On the cross," he replied. "He cried out, 'My God, my God, why have You forsaken me?'"

"Carlos, you're correct that Jesus asked that question. How did the Father reply?"

"He didn't answer because He had turned His back on Jesus," Carlos answered.

That's a common viewpoint. Carlos made an assumption about the Father's reply to Jesus's question, but Carlos's assumption comes from his preexisting belief that Jesus had to satisfy the Father's justice by bearing His anger for our sin. This is an example of what I mentioned earlier—that our culture shapes the way we interpret the Bible. To Carlos, the Bible plainly says that God forsook Jesus.

Maybe that's what comes to your mind when I suggest that the Father didn't forsake Jesus on the cross. We have been taught that the question Jesus cried out is proof positive that the Father turned away from Him and abandoned Him in that moment. After all, we're told, "God can't look upon sin."

Separation Anxiety

In a moment I'll address the issue of God looking upon sin and the answer to Jesus's question. But first, consider this. If the Father separated Himself from the Son when Jesus became sin for us, what happened to the Trinity at that instant? The very essence of the Trinity is the shared interpenetration of life. In other words, the nature of the Godhead is the *loving oneness* known by the Father, Son, and Spirit. God is a Trinity. Speaking of God's core essence, we can't say where one person of the Trinity stops and the others begin because no such division exists. The Three-in-One is one in essence. When Christians speak of God, we are *always* referring to the Father, Son, and Holy Spirit. If it's not the Three-in-One, it is not the true and living God.

So if the Father separated from Jesus on the cross, literally forsaking Him and refusing to live in oneness with Him, the Trinity didn't exist at that moment. How could God exist if His unified, triune essence was undone? Considering that God *is* a Trinity, it would then be accurate to say that God no longer existed when Jesus was on the cross. God is no longer God? What an absurdity!

If God in His triune nature were to cease to exist for even one moment, reality would vaporize and vanish in an instant. "The Father was still in control," one might argue. But that doesn't solve the problem. Unless the Father, Son, and Spirit remain in union at every moment, everything comes to a screeching halt. God is a Trinity, and if the Trinity ceased to exist, God would cease to exist. And if God ceased to exist…goodbye everything.

The One who hung on the cross that day is the One who created and sustains this universe at every moment. "For by Him all things were created, both in the heavens and on earth, visible and invisible, whether thrones or dominions or rulers or authorities—all things have been created through Him and for Him. He is before all things, and *in Him all things hold together*" (Colossians 1:16-17). Separate Jesus from the Father at the cross, and we tear apart the fabric of the cosmos.

God in a Sinful World

The idea that God the Father can't look upon sin also leads to an insulting conclusion about Jesus, who is God the Son. He lived in this world in the very midst of sin. He not only looked upon it but even rushed toward people trapped in sin! He saw sin as a fatal disease that needed to be cured, not a legal violation that He needed to punish. So if Jesus rushed toward those caught in sin but His Father can't even look at it, what would that say about Jesus? Wouldn't it suggest that His level of purity was inferior to that of His Father? Our triune God isn't allergic to sin in the way Superman would avoid kryptonite. To the contrary, in Jesus, He dove right into the deep end of the pool of the human condition in order to heal us and free us from sin's death sentence against us.

Where did this idea that God can't look on sin begin? The idea actually began in the Garden of Eden when Adam hid after he sinned. He assumed he needed to hide because God must not see him now that he had sinned. What was God's response? He came looking for Adam.

Habakkuk 1:13 does say that God can't look on evil, but this verse deserves a closer examination than most people have given it. The prophet Habakkuk witnessed the people of Israel suffering evil at the hands of those who hated the God of Israel, and he couldn't make sense of it. He cried out to God, "Your eyes are too pure to look on evil; you cannot tolerate wrongdoing" (NIV).

Here is where we have to be careful in studying the Bible. When we read any statement in Scripture, we dare not lift it out of its context. This verse demonstrates how we can come to a wrong and damaging viewpoint if our study of a verse is weak and incomplete.

If we were to stop right there with what Habakkuk said (and many do!), we would be forced to conclude that God cannot look on evil (sin). After all, the Bible "plainly says it." But wait. Remember that we aren't to rush to what the Bible says to validate our beliefs. We need to know what the Scripture *means*. In this case, we can see how Carlos might come to a wrong solution.

1	Jesus cried out, asking why God forsook Him.
+1	Habakkuk said that God couldn't look on evil.
=3	God the Father forsook Jesus.

It is impossible *not* to reach a wrong conclusion when we misunderstand the first two variables. Carlos assigned a wrong value to Jesus's question—he mistook it for an answer. The fact that Jesus cried out does not mean God forsook Him.

What about what Habakkuk said? Look at the remainder of the verse and see this first part in context.

> Your eyes are too pure to look on evil;
> you cannot tolerate wrongdoing.
> *Why then do you* tolerate the treacherous?
> Why are you silent while the wicked
> swallow up those more righteous than themselves?

Do you see how the context of the first line changes its meaning entirely? Habakkuk said, "God, You can't look on evil or tolerate wrongdoing, so why are You doing that very thing right now?" He was expressing his bewilderment to God. Take note—God didn't tell Habakkuk that He couldn't look on evil. Instead, Habakkuk was venting his pain and confusion through prayer.

God's actions didn't fit Habakkuk's theology. He thought God's holiness kept Him from looking at evil. Where did Habakkuk get that idea? It had been passed down through the generations since Adam had thought the same thing. It was the result of Adam eating the forbidden fruit. When he did, the lights went out, and mankind's clear understanding became darkened.

Again, this is a matter of how we interpret the Scripture. Bring the wrong presupposition to it from the start, and it is impossible to come to the right answer. Some conclusions that unquestionably true are actually wrong because we started with faulty presuppositions.

Aren't you thankful that our God's grace is bigger than our misconceptions? He is good regardless of what we believe. God didn't act the way Habakkuk thought He should. Thankfully, He still doesn't always act the way we think He should. His nature is to love, and that is what He does. Of course, God *can* look on sin. Otherwise, how could He have looked at the people He created? Sin doesn't scare God. Jesus came to this world to face it, to defeat it, and to put it away once and for all.

What About the Main Question?

But we're still left with the fact that Jesus cried out, "My God, my God, why have You forsaken me?" What do we do with that? First, we recognize that the Gospels do not record the Father answering Jesus's question. Jesus uttered seven statements from the cross, but this is the only one mentioned in more than one Gospel. Both Matthew and Mark record this question, and neither Gospel indicates that God answers.

The Bible does provide an answer to Jesus's question, but before we look at it, we need to recognize the great value of this cry from Jesus's heart. At that moment, as the One who chose "to be sin for us" (2 Corinthians 5:21), He *felt* abandoned by God the Father. When we feel as if God isn't there when we need Him, when He doesn't seem to care about our circumstances, when we appear to be all alone with no hope of help, Jesus stands in solidarity with us. He understands the anguish of feeling forsaken by our heavenly Father. He knows the heartache, the confusion, and the turmoil of feeling ignored by the One who defines Himself as pure love. He understands why we would ask, if the Father can help, why won't He?

So don't condemn yourself for having negative emotions at times when you face problems in life. Jesus stands with you even now, affirming your pain while gently reminding you of the answer He couldn't see in the instant He became sin for us. What is the answer to this question? "My God, my God, why have You forsaken me?" This isn't the first time the question is found in the Bible. The Old Testament includes some messianic psalms—songs that speak specifically about the coming of the Messiah, who was to redeem His people. These psalms weren't just songs of hope. They were songs of promise. They were prophecies about Jesus and what He would do when He came to this world.

Psalm 22 is one of the most easily understood psalms about Jesus because its meaning is so obvious. The very first verse of this psalm records the question Jesus would cry out a thousand years later. "My God, my God why have You forsaken me?" It must be an important question because it is the first thing the Holy Spirit inspires the psalmist to write in this psalm.

> All who see me sneer at me;
> They separate with the lip, they wag the head, saying,
> "Commit yourself to the Lord; let Him deliver him;
> Let Him rescue him, because He delights in him" (verses 7-8).

Compare this description with the Gospel accounts, and you will see that it happened exactly the way this passage describes.

> They open wide their mouth at me,
> As a ravening and a roaring lion.
> I am poured out like water,
> And all my bones are out of joint;
> My heart is like wax;

It is melted within me.
My strength is dried up like a potsherd,
And my tongue cleaves to my jaws;
And You lay me in the dust of death.
For dogs have surrounded me;
A band of evildoers has encompassed me;
They pierced my hands and my feet.
I can count all my bones.
They look, they stare at me;
They divide my garments among them,
And for my clothing they cast lots (verses 13-18).

Could this describe any better what Jesus experienced on Golgotha? Right down to the casting of lots for His garment, this prophetic psalm gives meticulous detail. Is it obvious to you that this psalm is a detailed explanation of what happened at the cross? Could it be more specific? I think not. So what about the question Jesus cried out, which is cited in the first verse of this psalm?

"My God, my God, why have You forsaken me?" Verse 24 gives a clear answer to the question.

For He has not despised nor abhorred the affliction of
    the afflicted;
Nor has He hidden His face from him;
But when he cried to Him for help, He heard.

Do you see the answer in this verse? Just as surely as the other verses in this prophetic psalm about the crucifixion of Jesus describe exactly what happened there, so verse 24 gives the exact answer to the question Jesus cried out in the Gospel narratives.

Did the Father turn away and hide His face from Jesus? "Nor has He hidden His face from him," the prophecy assured. Did the Father absent Himself and ignore Jesus when He cried out from the cross? "When he cried to Him for help, He heard."

If we come back to the biblical equation about the meaning of the cross, it should now look like this.

1	Jesus only *felt* as if God the Father had abandoned Him.
+ 1	Habakkuk's statement that God couldn't look upon sin showed his own faulty understanding.

= 2	God the Father never forsook His Son on the cross, but was with Him the whole time.

If we view God as a judicial deity whose sense of justice forced Him to punish Jesus for our sin, we will certainly believe that He abandoned His Son at the cross. But this clear answer in Psalm 22:24 can empower you to change your mind about the matter and move beyond an angry God to an understanding of your loving Father as He really is and always has been.

The moment Jesus became sin for you and cried out to His Father, He didn't hear an answer. But now you know the answer because it's plainly given in this messianic psalm. This was the Father's answer: "I hear You. I haven't forsaken You. I am with You, *in You* as You go through this. I will bring You out on the other side into resurrection life." The beauty of the Father's answer is that it wasn't only to Jesus. It is His answer to you when you face the dark moments of life. Your Father isn't angry toward you. He loves you and will be with you regardless of what you face in life.

You, too, may feel forsaken, but you are not. When you cry to the Father for help, He hears. He has not hidden His face from you. Trust Him even when you can't see Him, when you feel abandoned, and when you want to cry out, "Why?"

Old Testament Types

If I asked you to name the clearest Old Testament picture of Jesus's death for us on the cross, what would you choose? You would probably say that the Old Testament sacrifices are the clearest picture of what He did on the cross, and you would be right. Nothing in the Old Testament Scriptures gives us a clearer foreshadowing of what Jesus was to do in His death.

The Bible calls the Law system of sacrifices "a shadow of the good things to come" (Hebrews 10:1). A shadow is an image caused by light passing over a material object. The object is the true substance; the shadow is just a likeness.

The Old Testament sacrifices certainly couldn't do everything Jesus did when He offered Himself. The Bible says about Him, "By one offering He has perfected for all time those who are sanctified" (Hebrews 10:14). So the Old Testament sacrifices can't possibly be as valuable as what He did.

Those sacrifices can, however, show us something important about Jesus's sacrifice on the cross. They reveal that it had nothing to do with an angry God who was punishing His Son. Examine every reference to sacrifices under the Mosaic system in the Old Testament, and you will not find a shred of evidence of anger or a single reference to punishment.

Consider the most well-known Old Testament sacrifice—the Passover lamb. The apostle Paul plainly said this lamb pointed to Jesus (1 Corinthians 5:7). Was this lamb punished in anger? Not in any sense.

After choosing a lamb to be sacrificed for a Jewish household, the family brought it into their home to live with them for four days prior to the sacrifice. In fact, Jewish tradition tells us they would name the lamb, essentially making it a family pet—playing with it and nurturing it. All of this was done to assure that each family member would feel a personal connection to the lamb (see Exodus 12:3,6).

When the day came for the lamb to be sacrificed, the occasion wasn't marked by anger. Instead, it was a solemn experience. The gravity of the situation was defined by its significance and not by an angry outburst. In fact, the ceremonial slaying of the lamb was done in a humane way. Often the neck of the lamb would be shaved until the skin was completely bare. The blade would be sharp, and with one swift slice across the throat of the animal, it was finished. No anger or cruelty was intended or expressed in the process. The sacrifice was effective because of the blood of the lamb, not because of any violence, anger, or punishment.

The Scapegoat

The Day of Atonement was one of the most important occasions in Israel. Jews no longer offer sacrifices, but Yom Kippur (the Day of Atonement) is still the most holy day of the year for Jewish people. In modern times the day is marked by fasting, prayer, and synagogue services, but in biblical days the highlight of the day was the offering of the scapegoat. Leviticus 16 describes how the priest fulfilled this duty.

> He shall take the two goats and present them before the LORD at the doorway of the tent of meeting. Aaron shall cast lots for the two goats, one lot for the LORD and the other lot for the scapegoat. Then Aaron shall offer the goat on which the lot for the LORD fell, and make it a sin offering. But the goat on which the lot for the scapegoat fell shall be presented alive before the LORD, to make atonement upon it, to send it into the wilderness as the scapegoat...
>
> When he finishes atoning for the holy place and the tent of meeting and the altar, he shall offer the live goat. Then Aaron shall lay both of his hands on the head of the live goat, and confess over it all the iniquities of the sons of Israel and all their transgressions in regard to all their sins; and he shall lay them on the head of the goat and send it away into the wilderness by the hand of a man who stands in readiness. The goat shall bear on itself all their iniquities to a solitary land; and he shall release the goat in the wilderness (verses 7-10,20-22).

Today, the word *scapegoat* describes somebody who takes the blame for someone else's wrongdoing. The scapegoat in the Mosaic sacrificial system did just that. Aaron, the priest, would lay his hands on the head of the goat and confess the sins of the people, thus transferring all their sins onto this sacrifice. Then the goat would be led into the wilderness and released, carrying away the sins of the people.

This goat was clearly an Old Testament picture of Jesus. It depicted what Jesus would do with our sins. Now consider this—was the goat punished in anger?

This goat indeed pointed to the work Jesus was to do in dealing with our sin. The goat was not punished by an angry priest but simply took the sins of the people on itself and carried those sins away. This is exactly what Jesus did for us. By the power of the Spirit and in the presence of His Father, He took our sin and carried it away from us. Hebrews 9:26 says that He "put away sin by the sacrifice of Himself." Just as Aaron wasn't angry when he laid his hands on the head of the goat, neither was our Father angry when Jesus took away the sins of the world.

The Sin Offering

Leviticus 5 describes the sin offering, which provides perhaps the clearest demonstration that the Father was not punishing Jesus on the cross.

> So it shall be when he becomes guilty in one of these, that he shall confess that in which he has sinned. He shall also bring his guilt offering to the LORD for his sin which he has committed, a female from the flock, a lamb or a goat as a sin offering. So the priest shall make atonement on his behalf for his sin.
>
> But if he cannot afford a lamb, then he shall bring to the LORD his guilt offering for that in which he has sinned, two turtledoves or two young pigeons, one for a sin offering and the other for a burnt offering. He shall bring them to the priest, who shall offer first that which is for the sin offering and shall nip its head at the front of its neck, but he shall not sever it. He shall also sprinkle some of the blood of the sin offering on the side of the altar, while the rest of the blood shall be drained out at the base of the altar: it is a sin offering. The second he shall then prepare as a burnt offering according to the ordinance. So the priest shall make atonement on his behalf for his sin which he has committed, and it will be forgiven him.
>
> But if his means are insufficient for two turtledoves or two young pigeons, then for his offering for that which he

has sinned, he shall bring the tenth of an ephah of fine flour for a sin offering; he shall not put oil on it or place incense on it, for it is a sin offering. He shall bring it to the priest, and the priest shall take his handful of it as its memorial portion and offer it up in smoke on the altar, with the offerings of the LORD by fire: it is a sin offering. So the priest shall make atonement for him concerning his sin which he has committed from one of these, and it will be forgiven him; then the rest shall become the priest's, like the grain offering (verses 5-13).

The instructions here were for a person to bring an offering for sin. He was to bring a lamb or goat unless he didn't have one. In that case he could bring two turtledoves or pigeons. If he was so poor that he couldn't even bring that, then he could bring a basket of fine flour and use it as an offering.

Students of the Bible know that like the other sacrifices, this was a picture of Jesus. How, then, could an ephah of flour perfectly represent Jesus if a necessary component of His sacrifice was to receive angry punishment from God the Father? It would be ridiculous for the priest to have demonstrated anger toward a basket of flour!

The fact is, nothing in the Old Testament sacrifices points toward an angry God pouring out anger against His Son for our sins. To the contrary, the New Testament reveals just the opposite. Paul wrote to those at Ephesus, "Be imitators of God, as beloved children; and walk in love, just as Christ also loved you and gave Himself up for us, an offering and a sacrifice to God *as a fragrant aroma*" (Ephesians 5:1-2). Jesus's sacrifice didn't cause His Father to turn away in disgust—it was actually a beautiful smell that brought the Father great joy as He witnessed the selflessness of His Son.

A Troubling Tradition

If Jesus had to die to satisfy God's justice, as modern Western theology has suggested, then troubling questions remain. First, how can it be said that the Father forgave me (in the way the word is commonly used) for a debt I owed Him if the debt was actually paid? If you owed me $1000 and a generous friend of yours paid me what you owed, how would you respond if I came to you and said, "I've forgiven your debt"? You would remind me that I hadn't forgiven anything but that the debt had been paid on your behalf.

Additionally, if one insists on using a judicial understanding of justice to interpret the cross, how would that scenario even make sense? Would justice be served if a judge punished an innocent person in the place of the guilty party? If someone murdered my loved one and a legal ruling ordered the murderer's family member to be put to death, would that serve justice?

Consider the word *forgiveness*. It doesn't have to have the judicial meaning we often assume it does. It can also mean "to take away." The Old Testament was written in the Hebrew language, and the word most commonly translated *forgive* is *nasa*, which means to pick something up and carry it away.[2] For example, Psalm 32:1 says, "Blessed is he whose transgression is *forgiven*, whose sin is covered." The word used there is *nasa*. It is translated "forgive" eight times in the Bible, but it can also be translated in other ways.

For instance, when Nehemiah was about to go into King Artaxerxes's presence, he "took up [*nasa*] the wine and gave it to the king" (Nehemiah 2:1). When God reminded Israel of His faithfulness, He said, "You yourselves have seen what I did to the Egyptians, and how I bore [*nasa*] you on eagle's wings, and brought you to Myself" (Exodus 19:4). When Jonah found himself in the boat with the others and they were all about to die in a storm because of his sin, he said to them, "Pick me up [*nasa*] and throw me into the sea" (Jonah 1:12). The list could go on and on because the word is used 611 times in the Old Testament.

What about forgiveness in the New Testament? Two Greek words (the original language of the New Testament) are translated *forgive*. The first is *aphiemi*, which means "to send or make go away."[3] The word is used 133 times and, like the Old Testament Hebrew word *nasa*, it indicates that something is taken away.

The word is used in 1 John 2:12: "I am writing to you, little children, because your sins have been forgiven you for His name's sake." John was saying that through the cross, our sins have been taken away.

The tense of the verb indicates that the result will be ongoing—our sins have been forever sent away. It's not about an angry God deciding to move past His anger over our sins. The other New Testament Greek word translated *forgive* is *charizomai*. The root of the word is *charis*, which means "grace." It is used 19 times in the New Testament and denotes the action of doing something pleasant, gracious, and benevolent toward another person.[4]

Jesus's death was the source of the forgiveness of our sin, but I hope you can see that at the crucifixion, the Father didn't pour out His anger on Jesus in order to satisfy a kind of justice that demanded payback. Neither is His forgiveness mere exoneration for crimes we have committed. Rather, divine forgiveness is the gracious act of sending our sins away from us and never associating them with us again.

If the Father didn't punish Jesus on the cross, does that mean there is no punishment for sin? No, it doesn't mean that at all. There is indeed a punishment for sin, but it doesn't come from Pure Love. Sin brings its own punishment.

Chapter 6

God Isn't Angry

"So you're saying that Jesus didn't take the punishment for our sins on the cross?" Blake asked me.

"No, I'm not saying that at all. Jesus did take our place on the cross, and He certainly was punished. But the punishment didn't come from His Father," I answered.

"Then who *did* punish Him if it wasn't His Father?" he continued, seeming mildly frustrated.

"Blake, the reason for your frustration about this is your insistence that sin is a crime that deserved to be punished by God as if He were a cosmic prosecuting attorney."

After a few weeks of ongoing conversation and study, Blake said to me one day, "I get it. I've always viewed God as holy in the sense that He had to punish in some way. But the fact is, He doesn't look at us that way. He sees us as a loving father would. He had to deal with our sin, or it would destroy us."

It was a great joy for me to see him come to this understanding. From the time Adam sinned and hid himself in the Garden of Eden, people have had the mistaken notion that God was coming to exact revenge on them for their wrongdoing. When we begin to see our Father through the eyes of grace, we understand that the cross wasn't a courtroom. Rather, Jesus sacrificed Himself for us by taking our sin into Himself so we could be healed from its deadly effect.

Paul wrote, "The wages of *sin* is death" (Romans 6:23). God doesn't execute a death sentence on those who sin. Sin itself does that. Remember, God didn't tell Adam He would kill him if he ate from the forbidden tree. He told him that in the day he ate from that tree, he would surely die. But it would be *sin* that caused him to die, not his loving Creator.

What About Propitiation?

During our weeks of study together, Blake wrestled with the subject of propitiation. We don't use that word every day, but it is inseparably connected to any study of Christ's atonement. In Romans 3:25, the apostle Paul refers to Jesus as the One "whom God displayed publicly as a propitiation in His blood through faith."

The word has often been used to denote an appeasement for sin in a punitive sense. One Greek lexicon defines the word as "relating to an appeasing or expiating, having placating or expiating force, expiatory; a means of appeasing or expiating."[1] At first pause, the word could certainly suggest the sort of act that makes Jesus the recipient of retribution from His Father, especially if our minds are already hardwired to see the Father as an angry God who needed to vent.

However, there is another way to see the word *propitiation*. The Greek lexicon further says it is "used of the cover of the ark of the covenant in the Holy of Holies, which was sprinkled with the blood of the expiatory victim on the annual Day of Atonement."

This leads us to interpret Romans 3:25 in a way that is consistent with 1 John 4:8 ("God is love"). Note that this aspect of its meaning refers to the mercy seat that covered the Ark of the Covenant. On the Day of Atonement, the high priest anointed the mercy seat with blood from the sin offering to make atonement for the holy place for another year (Leviticus 16:14-16).

Remedy or Retribution?

So the word *propitiation* is used not only to refer to expiation in a judicial sense but also to refer to a place—the place where sin was dealt with by the blood of a sacrifice. In the Septuagint (a Greek translation of the Hebrew Old Testament), the Hebrew word *kaporeth* ("mercy seat") is translated *hilasterion* ("propitiation"). So they obviously held the view that propitiation had more to do with the remedial aspect of the sacrifice for sin than it did for any sort of retribution exploding out of an angry Father upon His Son. The propitiation was the place where sin was dealt with. In other words, the cross was the New Covenant substance foreshadowed by the Old Covenant mercy seat.

God didn't pour out anger against Jesus on the cross, just as the Old Testament high priest didn't pour out anger against a lamb on the mercy seat. Propitiation was remedial, not retributive! The cross was the place of divine agape, not divine anger! The only anger at Calvary was the anger of sinful humanity unleashed on Pure Love.

The cross of Jesus Christ is the purest expression of love that has ever existed or will ever exist. In that place of propitiation, as Pure Agape submitted Himself to the ferocity of sinful humanity, He also absorbed our sin into His own body and soul so that we would be delivered from its consequence.

Your God wasn't angry with Jesus, and He isn't angry with you. He never has been. The cross proves that. If He died for us while sin stubbornly held onto us and we held onto sin, you can be assured that He loves us now (see Romans 5:8). Religion has smeared His face with mud from the garden of guilt after the fall of man, but that false image doesn't negate the reality of who He is at all. "God is love." He always has been and always will be.

The Cross Dealt with Sins

If the Father didn't pour out His anger on Jesus at the cross, then what exactly did take place there? The truth will lead you to appreciate the death of Jesus more than you ever could before. What did Jesus do at the cross? And how have we found ourselves today in this place where so many wrongly think that God the Father was punishing His Son in anger on the cross?

To answer that question, we have to go back to the early church. For the first 1000 years of church history, believers saw the cross as the place where Jesus defeated sin so we would no longer be its prey. He took the toxic, deadly sin of the world into Himself and paid the ultimate price so we would be delivered from the death sentence sin brings. In doing so, He successfully freed us (humanity) from the tyranny of sin over us. He did what He came to do—take it away (see John 1:29; Hebrews 9:26; 1 John 3:5). Today this viewpoint is called *Christus victor*, or in English, Christ the victor. Jesus Christ was victorious over sin, conquering it through His death and resurrection.

The idea that the Father punished Jesus didn't come along until later. It sprouted on the landscape of church history early in the eleventh century and came to full bloom about 400 years later. It started when Anselm, a Benedictine monk who went on to become the archbishop of Canterbury, wrote a book suggesting that God needed to be repaid for our sins. [2]

Anselm lived during medieval times, when the feudal system prevailed in society. It was a culture of authority in which honor was the highest good. Honor each other, especially those in authority, or punishment and reparations must be made. If you were caught stealing a man's slave, you had to either pay him what the slave was worth or suffer the consequences. If you disrespected an authority, you had better figure out a way to make that right, or feudal justice would rain down on you with rigorous retribution.

So to Anselm, the big sin of mankind was "not to render his due unto God." [3] He proposed that since God is entitled to honor, and since mankind failed to properly honor Him, a debt was owed. How could anybody repay such a huge debt to God? Only a person who lived a life of perfect honor to God could pay the debt.

Of course, there was only One who could satisfy such a debt. Anselm contended that Jesus satisfied humanity's debt to the Father by both His perfect life and His sacrificial death. This view is now called the satisfaction theory, and it set the stage for what was to come 400 years later with the Reformation.

Anselm interpreted the work of the cross through the lens of medieval feudalism. John Calvin's background was the study of law. When he looked at the cross, he saw sin as a crime that deserved to be punished. Indeed, it *had* to be punished for justice to be served. The only appropriate answer was the death penalty. So Jesus came and was put to death in our place, satisfying the justice of the Father. Calvin, Luther, Zwingli, Melanchthon, and other leaders in the Reformation developed this penal substitution theory, and it is still the way most of the Western church understands the cross.

As we saw in chapter 4, our Father's sense of justice doesn't demand that somebody has to be punished. The Father of Love isn't a divine bookkeeper who keeps a running tally of the debt we owe him. Neither is He a district attorney who watches our behavior and builds a case against us that has to be resolved by punishment.

At the cross, Jesus took away the sin that would destroy mankind. He defeated it "once for all" (Hebrews 10:10). The cross was not penal substitution. Rather, it was the precious solution our triune God had set in place before time began. Christ *is* victor over sin and has provided more for all people than most of the world even knows.

The Cross Dealt with Sinners

A couple of things happened at the cross. First, Jesus put away the sins humanity had committed. But if that were all Jesus had done, we would still have a big problem. Sins were the symptom of a deeper problem—man's sinfulness. Everybody is born into this world with the nature that was passed down from Adam. It is a fallen nature, doomed to produce sinful actions. What good would it do to deal with the fruit and leave the root intact?

So Jesus also had to do a second thing at the cross. Not only did the sins of Adam's race need to be put away, but Adam's race itself had to die. As long as the family of Adam continued to live, nothing else could happen other than sin. A sinful nature can produce nothing but sinful actions. Mankind didn't simply need to stop sinning. We needed the source of sin to be put to death. Cleaning up a flooded room does no good if you don't stop the leaking faucet.

So that is exactly what Jesus did. He took on Adamic humanity, drawing it into Himself on the cross so we would die with Him. Jesus wasn't the only one who died on the cross that day. You died with Him! The question is, who else was included—only believers, or does this act of Jesus on the cross include everybody?

The Bible answers this clearly. "The love of Christ controls us, having concluded this, that one died for all, therefore all died; and He died for all, so that they who live might no longer live for themselves, but for Him who died and rose again on their behalf" (2 Corinthians 5:14-15). For whom did Jesus die? Twice in this text, Paul wrote that He died for all.

Does *all* really mean everybody? Some suggest that the word *all* doesn't always mean everybody, and they are correct. The Bible sometimes uses the word in a generic sense. For example, the Bible says that all Judea went out to be baptized by John in the Jordan (Mark 1:5). Obviously, not everybody in Judea was baptized. The word there means, "all types of people."[4] It's like saying, "Everybody eats at that restaurant." We don't literally mean everybody. We're using the word in a general sense.

On the other hand, the word can also mean each and every person.[5] The question is, did Jesus die for all types of people or for each and every person? I believe the latter to be the case. The Scripture says, "But we see Jesus, who was made a little lower than the angels for the suffering of death, crowned with glory and honor; that he by the grace of God should taste death for every man" (Hebrews 2:9 KJV). He didn't just die for all kinds of people. Jesus tasted death for *every* person.

Look again at the verse in 2 Corinthians 5. "One died for all." Who is the One who died for all? That's Jesus. Who are the all? That's *everybody*.

Paul goes on to say, "Therefore all died." Is it the same all? Of course it is. The verse clearly teaches that the same ones for whom Jesus died are the ones who died with Him. Jesus died for Adam's race, and that same race (humanity) died with him.

When Did Sinful Humanity Die?

When did this happen? Does it happen when a person trusts Christ by faith? No, it doesn't. It happened at the cross. Faith in Christ makes a person experientially aware of what happened at the cross, but what He accomplished there is real regardless of whether we know it or believe it. *You* and *your decision* didn't cause your co-crucifixion with Christ. Jesus and His finished work accomplished that. Let's not say we believe that everything is centered in the cross and then turn around and contend that the cross means nothing until we believe it. Let the credit rest where it belongs—on Jesus.

Does this then mean everybody is a Christian? No, it doesn't. A Christian is a believer in Jesus Christ. Rather, it means that the success of the finished work of Jesus Christ on the cross doesn't depend on human beings casting a vote in His favor. When He cried out, "It is finished," He meant it. There is nothing we need to do to deal with the problem of sin. Jesus has already done it. All need only to believe it and receive it so that our experience aligns with the eternal reality of His successful work on our behalf.

Our sins and our sinful nature were both crucified with Him that day. We aren't included in the crucifixion of Jesus at the moment we believe. "I have been crucified with Christ" regardless of whether I have faith in Him. My belief doesn't make it real. Humanity's co-crucifixion with Jesus on the cross is real whether we believe it or not. Watchman Nee wrote, "It is the inclusive death of the Lord which puts me in a position to identify myself, not that I identify myself in order to be included. It is God's inclusion of me in Christ that matters."[6] Which, then, is the correct order? Do we believe and then become included in His death, or we are included and then believe?

Nee rightly answers that we are not included because we believe. We believe because we are included, and that is what matters. Faith doesn't make it happen. We died with Jesus, and the old Adamic nature was destroyed. It happened! We all died with Him—that's a historical fact regardless of whether we have faith. Faith doesn't manufacture anything. It simply sees what already exists and is real whether we see it or not. We all died with Jesus, and that is a fact. Consider how these translations of 2 Corinthians 5:14 all affirm this wonderful truth.

- "The love of Christ controls us, having concluded this, that one died for all, therefore all died" (NASB).

- "Christ's love compels us, because we are convinced that one died for all, and therefore all died" (NIV).

- "It is the love of Christ which is moving us; because we are of the opinion that if one was put to death for all, then all have undergone death" (BBE).

- "The love of Christ compels us, because we judge thus: that if One died for all, then all died" (NKJV).

- "The love of the Christ doth constrain us, having judged thus: that if one for all died, then the whole died" (YOUNG'S).

Can it be clearer than this? Did Jesus die for all, or didn't He? Did Jesus die for everybody, but only some people died with Him? Did He die for all people, but they only die with Him if they believe they died too? What does the Bible say? The Bible teaches that everybody for whom Jesus died also died with Him. The gospel of grace that the human race needs to hear is that Jesus Christ has dealt with Adam's sin.

The Role of Faith   *I do not agree*

Remember that faith doesn't make anything happen. Faith is the evidence of things not seen (Hebrews 11:1). Those things are there already. They're just not seen. Through faith, the invisible reality that already exists becomes our visible experience. Through faith, the objective reality becomes our subjective realization.

Nothing is left for God to do for mankind. He has already done it all. To proclaim the gospel is to tell people that it really is finished. To experience salvation is to believe it and live from the reality of His work on our behalf. Thomas Torrance asserts this is true:

We must affirm resolutely that Christ died for all humanity—that is a fact that cannot be undone. All men and
women were represented by Christ in life and death, in his
advocacy and substitution in their place. That is a finished
work and not a mere possibility. It is an accomplished reality, for in Christ, in the incarnation and in his death on the
cross, God has once and for all poured himself out in love
for all mankind, has taken the cause of all mankind therefore upon himself. And that love has once and for all been
enacted in the substitutionary work on the cross, and has
become fact—nothing can undo it.[7]

Since Christ died for all humanity, all of us were included in his
death. As Torrance said, "That is a finished work and not a mere possibility." Remember that He didn't simply die for us; He also died *as* us.
Therefore, when He died, Adam's race died with Him.

Half truth

His Work Precedes Our Response

Does God do something for us based on what we decide to do, or is
our response based on something He has already done? Make no mistake about it—His loving work of grace precedes our response. We
aren't the first cause; He is. Consider Paul's announcement of the gospel in 2 Corinthians 5:19-20.

God was in Christ reconciling the world to Himself, not
counting their trespasses against them, and He has committed to us the word of reconciliation. Therefore, we are
ambassadors for Christ, as though God were making an
appeal through us; we beg you on behalf of Christ, be reconciled to God.

Carefully examine these verses word by word to answer these questions. Where was God the Father in relation to Christ when Jesus was
fulfilling His mission on our behalf? What was Christ doing on the
cross? Who were the intended beneficiaries of His crucifixion? Does
He count our sins against us? What is the exact message we have been
given to share with the world?

Did Christ Succeed?

Paul clearly states that God the Father was in Christ, not standing apart from Him and certainly not turning His back on Him. Jesus was reconciling the world to Himself through His sacrificial work. Did He succeed, or is the verdict still out on that? Of course He succeeded. The world has been reconciled to God. As ambassadors of Christ who speak as if God Himself were doing the talking, we spread this message: "You have been reconciled to God, and He doesn't hold your sins against you. Believe it! God has accepted you, so accept Him!"

Through the finished work of Jesus Christ, the sins of humanity have been forgiven (taken away). That's the best news we could ever receive! He didn't wait for us to do something first. Read the following description of the cross and consider these questions: What did Jesus do on the cross? When? What was the result? Did that result occur before we believed, or after?

> While we were still helpless, at the right time Christ died for the ungodly. For one will hardly die for a righteous man; though perhaps for the good man someone would dare even to die. But God demonstrates His own love toward us, in that while we were yet sinners, Christ died for us. Much more then, having now been justified by His blood, we shall be saved from the wrath of God through Him. For if while we were enemies we were reconciled to God through the death of His Son, much more, having been reconciled, we shall be saved by His life. And not only this, but we also exult in God through our Lord Jesus Christ, through whom we have now received the reconciliation (Romans 5:6-11).

Christ died for ungodly humanity "at the right time," says Paul. When was that time? It was "while we were still helpless," the Bible says. When did He demonstrate this love by dying for us? Verse 8 says it was "while we were yet sinners." When were we reconciled to God? Verse 10 says it was "while we were enemies" that He reconciled us to Himself through the death of this Son. None of these things happened after we believed. The Bible says the reconciling work of Christ happened while humanity was helpless, while we were sinners, and while we were enemies.

In light of this text, are we now going to turn around and face the opposite direction by insisting that people aren't reconciled and forgiven until they first believe? No, we believe because it has already happened. Our belief doesn't cause it to happen. We believe the gospel because it is already true, not so that it will become true. The overwhelming beauty of this kind of grace leaves us humbled, with only one decision to make—will we accept His acceptance?

In Victor Hugo's *Les Miserables*, Jean Valjean spends the night in the home of the bishop of Digne. Despite the bishop's generosity toward him, Valjean rises during the night and takes valuable silver from a cabinet. Hearing the noise, the bishop awakens and finds Valjean in the act of stealing his belongings. Valjean knocks him to the ground and flees.

Later in the day, the police arrive at the rectory with Jean Valjean in handcuffs. "He claims that you gave him the silver," one policeman scoffs.

"Yes, of course I gave him the silverware," replies the priest. "Valjean, why didn't you take the candlesticks too? They are worth at least two thousand francs." Turning to Madam Gilo, the bishop orders, "Go and fetch the candlesticks. And offer these men some wine. They must be thirsty."

Left alone together, the bishop holds Jean Valjean by the shoulders and looks deeply into his eyes. Valjean is confused. Speaking softly through restrained emotion, he asks, "Why are you doing this?"

The bishop answers with passion, "Jean Valjean, my brother, you no longer belong to evil. With this silver I've bought your soul. I've ransomed you from fear and hatred, and now I give you back to God."

With tear-filled eyes and an expression of disbelief, Valjean stands before the priest, speechless. [8]

Forgiveness. It is a troubling concept to the morality policemen of this world. In the rigid world of morality, meticulous records are kept to calculate the debt one owes. But in the land of grace, moral accounting is done away with, the books are burned, and record keeping is declared taboo.

Jean Valjean is all of mankind. We have been ransomed, and our sins have been forgiven. God has destroyed the record of our wrongdoing. It simply no longer exists. He has "canceled the certificate of debt consisting of decrees against us" and has forgiven everything we owe (see Colossians 2:13-14).

What Is Our Response?

What are we to do with such news? Simply acknowledge the love and forgiveness God has bestowed on us and accept it. We owe Him nothing, for grace is a gift that cannot be repaid.

This isn't true only for the world at large. Personalize this in your own life. Have you done something that gnaws at your conscience and causes you to feel guilty? Here's the good news inherent in the gospel—your sins have been forgiven. You owe God nothing for the things you have done. In Christ, God has taken your sin into Himself and eternally disposed of it.

The announcement of the grace of God is the incredible news that your sins are gone, and the sin-manufacturing nature you once possessed is gone too. He wants you to accept His acceptance and to let go of shame and tormenting regret.

God wants you to live without self-consciousness about anything you've done to dishonor Him. He has taken the dishonor of your sin upon Himself, and it is no longer yours to bear. To wallow in ongoing remorse about sin is to express the worst sort of insult toward God, the One who has removed your sins as completely as if you had never committed them in the first place. You are free, and God accepts you at this very moment. Believe it!

To paraphrase the words of the priest to Jean Valjean, Jesus has declared to you, "You no longer belong to evil and are no longer guilty. With my blood I've bought your soul. I've ransomed you from fear and hatred and have given you back to God."

Like Jean Valjean, you may stand speechless in total awe. The news of the gospel of grace may seem almost too good to be true, but believe it. Don't express contempt for Jesus's crucifixion by insisting on carrying the shame of the sins you have committed. Don't despise what He has done for you by refusing to gladly accept the forgiveness He has given. Affirm the reality that your sins are gone, never to be mentioned again.

Live in the joyful freedom that only those who have embraced their forgiveness can know. Don't listen to even a whisper of self-condemnation that may try to find a place in your thoughts. Reject it immediately by thanking God that what He accomplished at the cross on your behalf is indeed sufficient. He did what He did for you *before* you could do a thing or could even want to. He has received you, so relax and rest in His acceptance. You have been reconciled to God, so stop resisting Him and be reconciled to Him. In other words, own it and live in the freedom of divine acceptance and forgiveness of sin.

Why Do We Sin?

"If Jesus did that for the whole world, why do people still sin?" Owen asked me. "If the sin nature was taken away from everybody, why is the world still filled with sin?"

"Let me answer your question with a question," I responded. "Adam didn't have a sin nature before the fall in the Garden of Eden. Why did *he* sin?"

The reason Adam sinned and the reason people still sin today (both believers and unbelievers) is simple. They believe a lie. What is this lie? It is the lie that we can meet our own needs by relying on ourselves instead of living in dependence on our God. It is the lie that independence is a good thing. It is the lie that sinful behavior is gratifying and personally beneficial for those who sin.

Owen wrestled with the whole idea that the benefits from what Jesus did on the cross happened *then* and not when we express faith. To Owen, it wasn't really finished when Jesus died. It is finished only when we say it is by believing. *We* decide whether the cross was a success by our decision about Christ.

"But Jesus told the Pharisees that they were of their father, the devil," Owen protested.

. "That was *before* Jesus went to the cross and reconciled the world to God," I answered.

"But Paul talked about 'children of wrath,'" he insisted.

"You're right, but what does that mean?" I asked.

"It means God is going to punish them," he replied.

Let's pause here for a moment and consider Owen's concept of wrath. His belief is pervasive among those who haven't moved beyond the idea of an angry God. Owen still sees God as a punitive judge whose justice must be satisfied through revenge. Is that really what wrath means?

God's Wrath

The very mention of the phrase *the wrath of God* often brings to mind images of boils and pestilence and captivity. It is easy to associate it with a sudden violent outburst of anger directed against an offender. Does God explode with rage and revenge against those He has created? Does He reach a tipping point where loving concern finally falls aside and we see a side of Him about which Jesus didn't even give a hint? Does His love finally run out?

That was what Adam thought in the Garden of Eden after he sinned. He thought that surely God's attitude had changed and that His wrath and divine anger would rain down on him. But that's not what the wrath of God looks like at all. Due to Adam's sudden spiritual blindness, he didn't realize that the problem didn't reside in God but in himself. Norman Grubb explains.

> The wrath of God is only manifest in those who have the wrong relationship to Him. It is not Him as He is, who is all love. But it is what He must appear to be to those who run counter to the law of His being. The wrath operates in them, not in Him. If I have a right relationship to an electric switch and turn it on as I should do, I get a pleasant light. But if I defy any warnings and stick my finger in the apparatus, I get a nasty shock. The shock is what I feel within myself through my unlawful contact. So it

was not God who hid from the disobedient couple, it was they who hid from Him. They projected on Him a rejection which was really in themselves. And this is the wrath of God. All He said was, "Where are you, Adam? Come out from your hiding, I haven't changed." And when they came, He talked with them, not in judgment and wrath, but in mercy. All He told them was that they would experience the inevitable effects of the discords self-loving self always brings on itself.[9]

The word *wrath* certainly can denote an expression of anger, but does it mean that in every instance? Is that what it means when we refer to God's wrath? Again, as was the case with justice, there is another way to understand this concept that is perfectly consistent with the Bible.

There are two Greek words for wrath in the New Testament. The first is *thumos*.[10] This word is clearly associated with anger. It is used in the New Testament eighteen times. Ten of those are in the book of Revelation, and seven of those ten are references to the wrath of God (Revelation 14:10,19; 15:1,7; 16:1,19; 19:15). Are love and anger mutually exclusive? Any married couple can answer that question with a resounding no!

Is God's anger in the apocalyptic use of the word in Revelation disassociated from His love? It can't be, because God's nature is love and will always be love. Out of the eighteen times the word *wrath* is used in a way that denotes anger, it is used seven times in a book of the Bible that warrants much study before we come to a conclusion that God is mad at those who don't love Him. The book of Revelation contains hardly enough evidence to justify the kind of widespread view that pollutes the religious world today, one of an angry deity whose fury can only be satisfied by payback. God may be angry at sin, but you can rest assured He isn't angry with those trapped in it.

The other word that is translated as *wrath* in the New Testament is the word *orge*.[11] It is the most common word translated *wrath*, appearing 34 times. One definition of the word is "anger" or "temper," but there is more than one way to understand it.[12] Another meaning of the word is "movement or agitation of the soul, impulse, desire." Wrath usually refers to anger, but it can also refer to any violent emotion.

The word is in the same family as the ancient Greek word *orgia*, which means "secret rites" and is associated with the worship of pagan deities. It typically involved frenzied singing, dancing, drinking, and sexual activity. The word *orgia* is best translated into English as *orgies*, but what it shares in common with the word *orge* is that both are derived from the ancient Greek verb *orgao*, a word that denotes being eager. The point here is that wrath can have to do with passionate eagerness just as it does anger.

If a dad saw his young son standing in the yard holding a poisonous snake, the dad would run to him immediately. He would probably be shouting as he ran. The expression on his face and the tone of his voice might cause the child to become afraid, thinking his dad was angry with him. When the dad reached the boy, he may pick him up and begin to shake him, even slapping at his hand in an effort to make him drop the snake. The young child could easily think that his father was angry, even filled with rage.

Would that be the heart attitude of his father? It would not. The violent expression the child would see actually would be an expression of great passion *for* the son and *against* the snake. So it is with the wrath of our God. He is always for us and against everything that would destroy us. He hates sin—not because it does anything to Him, but because of what it does to those He loves. Don't ever allow yourself to think that God is against people, because He isn't. He is for us and will stop at no length to prove it.

Chapter 7

His Faith Changed Everything

Is your concept of God as an angry deity changing? We have seen that the very essence of God is love and that everything He does is motivated by love and not angry retribution. We have discovered that divine justice doesn't require somebody to be punished to satisfy God but instead makes things right for everybody involved. We have found that at the cross, the Father didn't pour out anger on His Son, Jesus. Rather, the Trinity was at work reconciling us all to God, not counting our sins against us. We have learned that the word *forgive* isn't to be understood in terms of a judge sitting in a cosmic courtroom passing a verdict against us. Instead, the word points to the fact that God has taken away our sins by drawing them into Himself on the cross. The message of the gospel is the story of divine love. Anything else pollutes the pure stream of grace.

This love is unconditional, unlimited, and unending. It is the reason Jesus came into this world as the God-man who lived, died, was buried, rose from the dead, and ascended back to the Father on behalf of each of us. History really is His story of love for all humanity as evidenced by the Incarnation. What He did was for everybody and not just for those who believe it.

> We all know that Jesus Christ died in our place on the cross; he took our place. But the vicarious humanity of Christ says that he took our place, not only on the cross, but he substitutes our entire human existence. He came to exchange humanities with us. He removed our alienated humanity and replaced it with real humanity—a humanity in face to face fellowship with the Father. The difference between speaking of the vicarious death of Christ and vicarious humanity of Christ, is in the first case Christ died in our place but in the second case, Christ lived, died, raised and ascended in our place, and remains in our place. Paul saw this vicarious humanity. He doesn't explain how it is possible nor does he theologize about it; he just sees it. One died for all therefore all died. Through Adam came condemnation and death to all, through Jesus came justification and life to all. In Adam we were emptied, in Jesus we have been filled.[1]

Do We Need to Believe?

Does that mean we don't need to believe the gospel? Absolutely not. But it does mean that Jesus was successful and His mission was effective regardless of how we cast our vote. As we have seen, we don't believe the gospel to make it true. We believe it because it *is* true.

Consider the following statements and ask, what is the truth?

1. A stunningly beautiful girl feels inferior and believes she is ugly.

2. An eccentric millionaire hoards his money under a mattress and lives as if he were poor.

3. A MENSA genius lacks social skills and feels stupid.

4. A little boy watching a scary movie is horrified that a monster is about to get him.

Is the girl beautiful or ugly? Is the millionaire rich or poor? Is the genius smart or stupid? Is the boy in danger or safe? Each of those four situations is defined by an objective, factual reality, but there is also a subjective, personal experience that cannot be ignored or denied. Each person's subjective experience contrasts with the objective truth.

The girl *is* beautiful, but until she believes it, her false belief will debilitate her. The millionaire *is* rich, but his money will do him no good whatsoever unless he appropriates the wealth that is already his. The genius *is* brilliant, but as long as he feels stupid, he won't enjoy social settings. The child is perfectly safe, but he will feel terror until he understands the truth.

In the same way, what Jesus did on the cross for all humanity is a reality that doesn't depend on our acknowledgment to be true. It's true whether we believe it or not. However—and this is important—until we believe the gospel, it will have no effect on our personal experience. Hebrews 4:2 makes this clear. "For we also have had the good news proclaimed to us, just as they did; but the message they heard was of no value to them, because they did not share the faith of those who obeyed" (NIV). The gospel is the same for both believers and unbelievers. It is the good news of what Jesus Christ has done for every one of us. The Bible says that unbelievers have been given the good news just as believers have, but "the message they heard was of no value to them." Why? It is because they did not share the faith of those who believed. Until a person believes the truth about herself, the gospel will make absolutely no experiential difference to her.

That doesn't mean what is true about her isn't still true. It simply means that she won't experience it. Just as the beautiful girl feels ugly and will be affected by those feelings, the unbeliever cannot enjoy the benefits of the work of the cross. That doesn't change what is real, but the impact on one's experience is immense.

Christians are those who believe the gospel of Jesus Christ and follow Him in faith. Not everybody is a Christian, but that doesn't mean that what Jesus did was a failure. Rather, it means that people won't experience and enjoy the reality of Christ's finished work if they don't believe it. Faith brings the eternal reality of His work into our temporal experience, but the work is already done, as theologian George Hunsinger explains.

> When God comes to humanity in the history of Jesus Christ, humanity at the same time is brought to God in that history objectively. It is not faith which incorporates humanity into Jesus Christ. Faith is rather the acknowledgment of a mysterious incorporation already objectively accomplished on humanity's behalf.[2]

Adam Isn't Bigger than Jesus

Think about what Adam did when he sinned. Did it affect everybody? Was there one person who wasn't affected by him eating from the forbidden tree in the Garden of Eden? We were all included in what he did that day. "When Adam sinned, sin entered the world. Adam's sin brought death, so death spread to everyone, for everyone sinned" (Romans 5:12 NLT). Nobody was exempt from Adam's disobedient deed in the Garden.

Jesus came into this world as "the last Adam" (1 Corinthians 15:45). Was Jesus's restoration project sufficient to repair the damage Adam had done? Was Adam bigger than Jesus? Jesus's obedient act encompassed all of humanity, just as Adam's disobedient deed did. Romans 5 continues, "Consequently, just as one trespass resulted in condemnation for all people, so also one righteous act resulted in justification and life for all people" (verse 18 NIV).

Adam's sin certainly was not greater than Christ's life and death. The effect of Jesus Christ's work extended every bit as far as the impact of Adam's sin. According to this verse, what did the work of Jesus Christ accomplish? Humanity was justified. Is Paul simply referring to all types of people—Gentiles as well as Jews—when he wrote these words? No, he is not comparing Jews and Gentiles. To insist that his comparison was between Jews and Gentiles is to inject something into the passage that the context doesn't warrant. Paul's comparison is between those affected by Adam's trespass and those affected by Christ's righteous act. It is a comparison between those Adam ruined and those

Jesus Christ redeemed. Consider how J.B. Phillps's translation renders the text from Romans 5:18: "We see, then, that as one act of sin exposed the whole race of men to God's judgment and condemnation, so one act of perfect righteousness presents all men freely acquitted in the sight of God." The comparison Paul had in mind included "the whole race of men."

Forgiveness and Faith

Consider the Old Testament sacrifices, which foreshadowed the way Jesus would offer Himself as a sacrifice for our sins. Were those sacrifices, which were offered by the priests under the covenant of the Law, equal to Jesus's sacrifice? They were not. To the contrary, they were far inferior. "For it is impossible for the blood of bulls and goats to take away sins" (Hebrews 10:4). The animal sacrifices in the Levitical system were much less effective than the finished work of Jesus Christ on the cross. Yet all of Israel's sin was covered by those inferior sacrifices. What Jesus did is much more far-reaching than were the sacrifices offered by priests in the Old Testament.

In that light, consider these questions. Did the Jewish person for whom the priest offered the sacrifice have to have faith in the sacrifice for his sins to be forgiven? Upon what was his forgiveness based? Whose faith that his sins would be covered was operating when the sacrifice was offered?

When the priest offered the sacrifice on the altar, Israel's sins were covered regardless of whether the people believed. That was true for everybody. Forgiveness was based on the purity of the sacrifice and had nothing to do with each individual's faith. The priest knew that the sacrifice was sufficient to cover their sins. *He* had faith in the efficacy of the blood of the animal. His obedience to God was sufficient to ensure that Israel's sins were dealt with in full.

In the same way, what Jesus did was for everybody. He was the perfect sacrifice who offered Himself for us before we could even respond with either faith or rejection. It was about His faithfulness and confidence in His Father. That was enough to accomplish what He came to do, which was to put away our sins by the sacrifice of Himself (see

Hebrews 9:26). He solved our sin problem before it even showed up, or for that matter, before *we* even showed up on earth. If the sacrifices offered by Old Testament priests were effective regardless of the people's response, then surely what Jesus did as both the High Priest and the Sacrifice were even more effective. Jesus's ministry in the New Covenant accomplished more than the priests' ministry in the Old Covenant ministry accomplished. The work of Christ is greater!

The core issue of the finished work of Jesus Christ on the cross isn't our faith, but His faithfulness. Although the contemporary emphasis is on our decision, the good news is really all about Him. Our faith is simply a joyful response to what He has already successfully done for us. It is finished regardless of what we do with it.

Whose Faith?

"But we have to have faith to be justified! Paul wrote that we are justified by faith," Ian told me after hearing me teach this truth.

"I agree," I replied. "Romans 5:1 says, 'Therefore, having been justified by faith, we have peace with God through our Lord Jesus Christ.' The question is, *whose* faith causes us to be justified?"

"Our faith in Christ," he responded.

Ian interpreted this verse the way most Evangelicals do today. He believed our faith in Christ is the catalyst for justification. This puts the burden on us to place our faith in Him in order to be justified.

That, however, is not what the Bible actually teaches, nor is it the view of the early church. Faith is indeed the conduit through which justification comes, but it's Jesus's faith that has justified us. It's not our own faith that we have placed in Him. He has justified us. He isn't waiting for us to do something so we can be justified through our own actions.

Two-Letter Words That Make a Huge Difference

Two pivotal words in this discussion of justification are *in* and *of*. To be justified by faith *in* Christ is very different from being justified by the faith *of* Christ. One depends on our faith, and the other rests in His faith.

I don't like His teaching it is dangerous

This is where we must take a serious look at what the Bible says and what it means. You can't just take somebody's word for it regardless of how much you respect that person. Sincere people who love Jesus are sometimes wrong. It is important that we all study the Bible to understand the truth. Translations vary from one another. That's why it is always important to compare translations when we study the Bible.

Consider how these translations differ in the way they approach this important matter of faith. As you compare the difference between the verses, ask yourself, does this translation suggest that the necessary faith originates with God or with man? As you know, grace always originates with God. It's not us giving Him something (such as our faith), but always a matter of Him giving us something. It is the unilateral expression of His love toward us. We could compare numerous translations, but I'll use two of the most popular translations that have endured the test of time—the King James Version and the New International Version. Remember to answer the question about whether the verse suggests that the faith necessary for justification originates with God or us.

Romans 3:22

The KJV translates this verse, "Even the righteousness of God which is by faith of Jesus Christ unto all and upon all them that believe: for there is no difference." Compare that with the NIV: "This righteousness is given through faith in Jesus Christ to all who believe. There is no difference between Jew and Gentile."

The righteousness of God comes by faith, but *whose* faith? The KJV says it is by the faith *of* Jesus Christ, but the NIV says it comes through faith *in* Jesus Christ. (A footnote in the NIV indicates the verse could be translated, "through the faithfulness of Jesus Christ.") Do you see how important this distinction is? The difference lies in whether the source of our righteousness is His faith or our faith.

Galatians 2:16

The KJV reads, "Knowing that a man is not justified by the works of the law, but by the faith of Jesus Christ, even we have believed in

Jesus Christ, that we might be justified by the faith of Christ, and not by the works of the law; for by the works of the law shall no flesh be justified." The NIV says, "[We] know that a person is not justified by the works of the law, but by faith in Jesus Christ. So we, too, have put our faith in Christ Jesus that we may be justified by faith in Christ and by works of the law, because by the works of the law no one will be justified."   *It is Both*

Again, are we justified by the faith *of* Christ or by putting *our faith in* Christ Jesus? The difference between the two is huge. How you answer the question will determine your theology in this area.

Galatians 2:20

The KJV renders this verse, "I am crucified with Christ: nevertheless I live; yet not I, but Christ liveth in me: and the life which I now live in the flesh I live by the faith of the Son of God, who loved me, and gave himself for me." The NIV renders it, "I have been crucified with Christ and I no longer live, but Christ lives in me. The life I now live in the body, I live by faith in the Son of God, who loved me and gave himself for me."

Again, whose faith is the catalyst for our righteousness—His or ours? It isn't *our* faith, but the faith of Jesus Christ that has made us righteous. We must not ignore an important principle in interpreting the Bible if we want to properly understand it. It is the Christocentric ("Christ centered") principle. The other way to interpret the Bible is the egocentric ("self-centered") approach. Which one do you believe is the best way to rightly understand the Bible? Look again at the verses in the paragraphs above and decide which translation approaches the verses from a Christ-centered approach and which takes the self-centered approach.

I'm not campaigning here for the King James Version, although I believe it is a wonderful translation. I'm simply making the point that we need to compare versions of the Scripture when we study. Don't think for a minute that translators didn't bring their own preconceived ideas to the text when they translated from the Greek or Hebrew into English.[3] That doesn't mean we can't trust our Bibles, but the fact is that we don't have the original manuscripts anymore, so it is always wise to compare translations. Too many of us have simply believed what we have been told for so long that we feel uncomfortable questioning it. But some things need to be questioned. In this case, the grace of God is impugned when we think *our* faith causes us to be justified.

Consistency Is Key

This importance of the distinction between the words *in* and *of* can further be seen in the way many translators handle two specific texts in Romans. Carefully notice the immediate context of the word *faith* in these passages. The first is Romans 3:25-26: "This was to demonstrate His righteousness, because in the forbearance of God He passed over the sins previously committed; for the demonstration, I say, of His righteousness at the present time, so that He would be just and the justifier of the one who has faith in Jesus." Take special notice of the phrase "faith in Jesus" in verse 26.

Now compare what Romans 4:16 says about faith: "For this reason it is by faith, in order that it may be in accordance with grace, so that the promise will be guaranteed to all the descendants, not only to those who are of the Law, but also to those who are of the faith of Abraham, who is the father of us all."

The first text refers to "faith in Jesus," and the second text mentions the "faith of Abraham." One verse uses the word *in*, and the other chooses the word *of*. Here is a perfect example of why so many have come to the wrong understanding about faith. Would it surprise you to know that Romans 3:26 and 4:16 use the same words, with the exception of the names Jesus and Abraham?[4] Only the names are different, and yet the verses are translated completely differently!

The NASB translators chose to render the reference to Jesus as "faith *in* Jesus," but they didn't translate the reference to Abraham as "faith in Abraham." Rather, they chose to rightly render it as "the faith *of* Abraham." If the NASB were consistent, Romans 3:26 would read, "for the demonstration, I say, of His righteousness at the present time, that He might be just and the justifier of the one who is of the faith *of* Jesus." (The NASB footnote offers this as an alternate translation.) The inconsistency here belies the bias of the translators. They wouldn't suggest that Paul was saying his readers should have faith *in* Abraham, but neither did they assert that we are justified by the faith *of* Christ. Their view was obvious—that we are justified by placing our faith *in* Christ.

Is It His Faith or My Faith?

The question is, is it *His* faith or *our* faith that matters? The answer is yes. It is both. His faith *becomes* our faith. Note how the apostle Paul explained it in Galatians 3:22 (KJV): "But the scripture hath concluded all under sin, that the promise by faith of Jesus Christ might be given to them that believe." The faith of Jesus Christ has taken away our sin, reconciled us to the Father, given us forgiveness, made us righteous, and many other things that we will consider later. Those benefits of the cross are objectively, factually true because of Him. When He said, "It is finished," He meant it! What is done is done.

However, Paul said the promise is given to "them that believe." This is believers' subjective, actual experience. Critics of this pure message of grace wrongly accuse those of us who hold this viewpoint as suggesting that it isn't necessary to believe, but that isn't true. It *is* necessary for us to believe that we are in right standing with God because of the finished work of Jesus Christ. But we believe it because Jesus has already accomplished it! We believe it to experience it.

Objective and Subjective Aspects of the Gospel

Both the objective (what God has done) and the subjective (what we believe and experience) aspects of the gospel are important. We can't marginalize or minimize either, but modern Evangelicalism places so much emphasis on our subjective faith that the objective faith of Christ is largely ignored. That is why I am emphasizing the objective component so strongly in this book.

Don't wrongly conclude that I think the subjective experience of personally embracing the finished work of Christ is unimportant. It is not only important but essential! However, we can believe only because of the faith of Jesus Christ that already stands as an eternal witness to the finished work of the cross. Our faith is the activation of His faith in and through us. There aren't two faiths—His and ours. There is only "one Lord, *one faith*, one baptism" (Ephesians 4:5).

Romans 1:17 says, "For in [the gospel] the righteousness of God is revealed from faith to faith; as it is written, 'But the righteous man shall live by faith.'" From faith to faith—what does that mean? It means that the faith of Jesus becomes our faith. When the apostle Paul wrote that the righteous man shall live by faith, he was pointing to Habakkuk 2:5, which clearly explains what Paul meant by his statement to the Romans. "But the righteous will live by *his* faith." It is absolutely correct to insist that our faith is important, but it is also absolutely essential to recognize that there would be no basis for our faith unless it was all sourced in Him. When we believe, we begin to live out in time what has been settled in eternity.

None Are Left Out

The atoning work of Christ doesn't affect us simply because we believe it. It affects everybody whether we believe it or not. That is what makes the gospel so exciting. No one is excluded in the cross. All mankind was in Him on that horrible, wonderful day.

Irenaeus of Lyon was a great theologian of the second century. He was a disciple of Polycarp, who had been a disciple of John. Here is his explanation of what Jesus did at the cross.

> Therefore, as I have already said, He caused man (human nature) to cleave to and to become, one with God. For unless man had overcome the enemy of man, the enemy would not have been legitimately vanquished. And again: unless it had been God who had freely given salvation, we could never have possessed it securely. And unless man had been joined to God, he could never have become a partaker of incorruptibility. For it was incumbent upon the Mediator between God and men, by His relationship to both, to bring both to friendship and concord, and present man to God, while He revealed God to man.[5]

John the Evangelist actually walked and lived with Jesus. Who did John's grandson in the faith believe was impacted by the finished work of the cross? Notice that he didn't say this only applied to those who believed it. Irenaeus plainly taught that what God did in Christ affected all humanity. His statement expresses the witness of the early church at large.

Move forward a few centuries, and Athanasius stands front and center in the church affirming what Irenaeus had said.

> Naturally also, through this union of the immortal Son of God with our human nature, all men were clothed with incorruption in the promise of the resurrection. For the solidarity of mankind is such that, by virtue of the Word's indwelling in a single human body, the corruption which goes with death has lost its power over all. You know how it is when some great king enters a large city and dwells in one of its houses; because of his dwelling in that single house, the whole city is honored, and enemies and robbers cease to molest it. Even so is it with the King of all; He has come into our country and dwelt in one body amidst the many, and in consequence the designs of the enemy against humanity have been foiled and the corruption of death, which formerly held them in its power, has simply ceased to be. For the human race would have perished utterly had not the Lord and Savior of all, the Son of God, come among us to put an end to death.[6]

When Jesus died, it was His faith (or to fine tune it even more, His *faithfulness*) that solved Adam's problem. All humanity was gathered up in Him, and in His death, we all died.

> Or do you not know that all of us who have been baptized into Christ Jesus have been baptized into His death? Therefore we have been buried with Him through baptism into death, so that as Christ was raised from the dead through the glory of the Father, so we too might walk in newness of life. For if we have become united with Him in the likeness of His death, certainly we shall also be in the likeness of His resurrection, knowing this, that our old self was crucified with

Him, in order that our body of sin might be done away with, so that we would no longer be slaves to sin; for he who has died is freed from sin.

Now if we have died with Christ, we believe that we shall also live with Him (Romans 6:3-8).

Scottish Bible teacher William Still commented on this passage.

There, Paul repeats the truth verse after verse in varying forms of words: we are "baptised into his death"; we are "planted together with him in the likeness of his death"; "our old man was crucified with him"; "he that is dead has been justified from sin"; we are "dead with Christ." Could anything be more plain? Paul says that when Jesus died, we died with him. The Negro spiritual is not wrong when it asks, "Were you there when they crucified my Lord?" We were all there.

But we must take time to ponder it. Does it mean that when Jesus died on the Cross we all died to sin with him, before we were born? The answer can only be, "Yes," although the actualizing of the fact awaits our birth and our conversion. The only way to grapple with the fact is to let its incredible statement strike home to our hearts with stark and daring force.[7]

Chosen Before We Believed

"We get right with God when we receive Jesus," Paula said. "We are taken out of Adam and placed into Christ when we believe."

"But what do you do with the apostle Paul's description of our origination in Him?" I asked her. "He says that we were chosen in Christ long before we believed in Him. In fact, Paul says we were chosen in Him before we were even born."

Here is the verse I read to Paula to make my point. Take special note of when this verse says that we were placed into Christ. "He chose us in Him before the foundation of the world, that we would be holy and blameless before Him" (Ephesians 1:4). The New Living Translation renders this verse, "Even before he made the world, God loved us and chose us in Christ to be holy and without fault in his eyes."

It wasn't our choice of Him that put us into Christ. It was His choosing us! We were chosen *in Christ* before anything was even created. When, then, do you find your origin in Christ? Was it when you prayed a prayer? Was it when you believed? No, your origin in Him precedes time and space, reaching all the way into eternity. Before one member of Adam's race showed up on this planet, even before the first taint of sin entered the world, our God had already chosen us in Christ and dealt with the problem of sin.

"So you're saying *everybody* is in Christ?" Paula asked incredulously.

"I'm not just saying everybody is in Christ. I'm saying *everybody and everything* is in Him," I replied.

Young's Literal Translation of Colossians 1:16-17 makes this clear.

> Because in him were the all things created, those in the heavens, and those upon the earth, those visible, and those invisible, whether thrones, whether lordships, whether principalities, whether authorities; all things through him, and for him, have been created, and himself is before all, and the all things in him have consisted.

The sentence structure is awkward in places, but the literal translation of the New Testament says that everything in existence was created *in Him*. Jesus Christ is the Creator and Sustainer of everything in existence. Look at the last phrase of verse 17: "the all things in him have consisted." Everything that exists is held together in Him. You can relax because you are at home in Him, and nothing exists or happens outside Him.

Living a Lie

I'm not suggesting that everybody has a conscious relationship to Christ, because they don't. But this verse clearly shows that everybody and everything is related to Him through a union about which they may or may not possess knowledge. He is "before all"—that doesn't refer to priority, but to placement. It refers to His immediate presence in the whole cosmos. There is no distance between God and man. Any perception of distance is an illusion caused by the whispering lies of ghosts from Adam's shadowy past, ghosts still haunting those who haven't seen the light of the gospel.

What happens when people don't know the truth of the gospel? They base their lives on this lie of separation. Paul described it, saying, "And you were dead in your trespasses and sins, in which you formerly walked according to the course of this world, according to the prince of the power of the air, of the spirit that is now working in the sons of disobedience" (Ephesians 2:2).

Without knowing the truth, humanity's default setting is to live the lie. Unbelievers are living out of a lie and not walking in the truth. The truth is that what Jesus did, He did for everybody, and its success doesn't depend on our agreement. It didn't happen when we believed but when we were still dead and incapable of believing. Ephesians 2:5-6 says, "Even when we were dead in our transgressions, [God] made us alive together with Christ (by grace you have been saved), and raised us up with Him, and seated us with Him in the heavenly places in Christ Jesus."

God's Work Came First

So which is it? Is it the work of Jesus Christ or the response of man that brings the benefits of the cross into existence? Grace would insist that His work and not our response to it gave birth to these things. Faith in Christ certainly links us to its reality, but there would be nothing to link us to if it weren't already real beforehand. We *are* reconciled, and that is why we can *be* reconciled (see 2 Corinthians 5:19-20). Theologian William Barclay helps us understand this.

> First and foremost, Paul sees the work of Jesus Christ as above and beyond all else a work of reconciliation. Through that which he did, the lost relationship between man and God is restored. Man was made for friendship and fellowship with God. By his disobedience and rebellion he ended up at enmity with God. That which Jesus did took that enmity away, and

restored the relationship of friendship which should always have existed, but which was broken by man's sin.

It is to be carefully noted that Paul never speaks of God being reconciled to men, but always of men being reconciled to God. The most significant of all the passages, 2 Corinthians 5:18-20, three times speaks of God reconciling man to himself. It was man, not God, who needed to be reconciled. Nothing had lessened the love of God; nothing had turned that love to hate; nothing had ever banished that yearning from the heart of God. Man might sin, but God still loved. It was not God who needed to be pacified, but man who needed to be moved to surrender and to penitence and to love.

Here then we are face to face with an inescapable truth. The effect of the cross—at least in this sphere of the thought of Paul—was on man, and not on God. The effect of the cross changed, not the heart of God, but the heart of man. It was man who needed to be reconciled, not God. It is entirely against all Pauline thought to think of Jesus Christ pacifying an angry God, or to think that in some way God's wrath was turned to love, and God's judgment was turned to mercy, because of something which Jesus did. When we look at it in Paul's way, it was man's sin which was turned to penitence, man's rebellion which was turned to surrender, man's enmity which was turned to love, by the sacrificial love of Jesus Christ upon the Cross. It cost that cross to make that change in the hearts of men.[8]

In Christ our God has reconciled the world to Himself. It isn't something we accomplish by our faith. It is simply a matter of receiving something that has already been done. Karl Barth elaborated on this point in his book *Christ and Adam*.

> In His own death He makes their peace with God— before they themselves have decided for this peace and quite apart from that decision. In believing, they are only conforming to the decision about them that has already been made in Him.[9]

This reconciliation He accomplished is the exchanged life. The biblical use of the word *reconciled* denotes the idea of exchanging coins for other coins of equivalent value. The full message of the exchanged life is that Jesus has exchanged the life of all of humanity with His own. In Romans 5:10 Paul affirms, "we were reconciled to God through the death of His Son." The word *reconciled* is used in a way that suggests this reconciliation happened *to* us because of God and is a reality that exists independent of anything we ever do or don't do. In fact, the word means it happened to us because of an outside force without us having done a thing. We are the objects of reconciliation, not the subjects.[10] This is true of every person for whom Christ died, which is every one of us, without exception. Regardless of whether we know it, believe it, or even like it, we are all included.

Our God isn't angry with us, because His acceptance of us isn't contingent on a proper response on our part. An improper response or no response to His love will undoubtedly impact our lives in negative ways that are too many to number, but that problem is on our end, not His. When we turn our attention to Jesus hanging on the cross for all humanity, we hear the passionate shout of Eternal Agape crying out in divine love for every one of us. We see the tangible evidence in space and time of the Trinity's resolve to reconcile every wandering soul into the warm embrace of a love that will never die.

Chapter 8

Not Your Grandmother's Hell

No book on the topic of an angry God could be excused for leaving out a consideration of hell. It is the definitive subject in the modern church that causes many to include God-sized anger in His character. The threat of hell has been the most widely used evangelistic weapon in the church for quite some time now. In contrast, the apostle Paul never used the word in all his epistles. Why should he? Paul had seen Jesus and could effectively describe Him. When we, too, have seen Jesus clearly and then present Him to others as He is, we don't need to scare people into heaven. Jesus will be enough to attract them.

When I preached hellfire and damnation, I used to say, "I'd rather scare them into heaven than see them go to hell!" But my zealous mantra narrowed everything down to two choices—to be scared into heaven or to go to hell. My argument missed the point.

I know now that salvation isn't about heaven and hell. It's about knowing our Father through His Son in the Holy Spirit. Jesus made that plain when He said, "This is eternal life: that they may know

You, the only true God, and Jesus Christ whom You have sent" (John 17:3). If you miss the beauty of God's love expressed in Jesus, your only evangelistic option is to try to scare people into faith. But when we truly know Him, we understand that His love is enough to entice people to Himself. Too many modern evangelistic efforts are still focused on threatening people with hell, "not realizing that God's kindness is intended to lead [them] to repentance" (Romans 2:4). The threat of hell is the approach often used in evangelism by folks who have never clearly seen the beauty of Jesus. Once we've seen Him, why would we focus on anything else in sharing the gospel?

People get nervous when they think anybody is minimizing hell, but I hope you'll see in this chapter that what I'm actually doing is maximizing the love of God! Don't jump to conclusions or think I'm going to say hell doesn't exist (it does) or that it should never be mentioned (it should). But my view may not be what you grew up hearing in church, for even our understanding of hell must be filtered through the lens of the love of our God.

There is a risk in writing a chapter like this one. The risk is great enough that I discussed with trusted advisors whether to even include it in the book. The danger is that the subject is such a volatile one that I was concerned that even to discuss it here might take away from the main theme I want to communicate. I hope that won't happen.

It's interesting that there can be a robust discussion among believers about the legitimacy of the gift of tongues, and nobody on either side sounds the heresy alarm. Christians can debate all day about the role of women in ministry, and at the end of the day everybody shakes hands and goes home. Calvinists who stand firmly on eternal security and Arminians who believe one can willfully forfeit salvation don't agree but still respect each other. Practically every subject you can think of allows space for civil discussion and debate. Differences of opinion are real. That's why an estimated 40,000 Christian denominations exist in the world today. People don't agree on everything, but disagreement on nonessentials has always been acceptable on the landscape of Christianity.

These days the subject of hell is another matter altogether. One doesn't have to deny the existence of hell to find himself in the cross-hairs of critics. Step away from a concept of hell as a place of literal fire where people are physically burned, and you run the risk of pitchforks and torches—and I don't mean after you die. Lock the gate because the mob will likely be coming.

My desire in writing this book is that the Teacher will change your mind about the nature of our Father, but this chapter isn't intended to convince you to have a different view of hell. My goal here is simply to stretch your thinking so you might recognize that there are varying ways to understand the *nature* of hell. Unlike some, I'm not suggesting that hell isn't real. Rather, I'm raising the issue of what we mean when we use the word.

Interestingly, only in recent years has this subject provoked such a firestorm of controversy. Throughout church history, the subject of hell has never been considered a core issue of the Christian's faith. Reach all the way back to some of the earliest writers in the church, and you'll discover that believers have always had widely diverse understandings of the nature of hell. To insist that our own understanding of what hell is like is *the* definitive stance reveals an undeniable cultural blindness.

The fact of the matter is that much of the imagery taught in the modern Evangelical church comes from outside the pages of Scripture. Ask the average churchgoer today to describe what hell is like, and you'll likely get a description that sounds much like Dante Alighieri's fictional account of hell in *Inferno*, one of three poems he wrote in The Divine Comedy. His writing describes his alleged experience in a three-day vision of a trip he took to hell, purgatory, and paradise in the year 1300. Then as now, the culture of entertainment shaped the way people thought about biblical topics. Dante's writing was so influential that some of his ideas continue to linger, shaping the way many people understand the nature of hell.

People may tell you that this subject has an ironclad interpretation, but they are basing their confident claim on their personal viewpoint. And in fact, the popular view has been questioned and disputed by serious Bible students and influential church leaders throughout history. It is not clear-cut and unanimously agreed upon and never has been.

Some people argue that hell is simply a figment of the imagination, a concept created by religious people to control others. As I'll explain shortly, some people argue that the Hebrew and English words translated *hell* in the Bible don't mean what we have been told they mean. On that point, I am in full agreement with them. However, I am not in agreement that there is no basis for believing in hell. I have reconsidered the nature of hell, but I stand solidly among those who affirm its existence. I agree with Robert Capon's words on this matter.

> I take with utter seriousness everything that Jesus had to say about hell, including the eternal torment that such a foolish non-acceptance of his already-given acceptance must entail. All theologians who hold Scripture to be the Word of God must inevitably include in their work a tractate on hell. But I will not—because Jesus did not—*locate hell outside the realm of grace.* Grace is forever sovereign, even in Jesus' parables of judgment. No one is ever kicked out at the end of those parables who wasn't included in at the beginning.[1]

The Current Conversation

Forgive my puns, but hell is a hot topic in the church today, and the ongoing debate is often inflammatory. Some people who love grace think we shouldn't even talk about the subject, but we need to address it because you can be sure everybody else is talking about it. If you doubt that, just check Facebook, scan popular blogs, or search the Internet to see how many books on the subject are out there. One man claims to have spent 23 minutes in hell, and others claim they've visited it numerous times. As a little exploration will reveal, this topic isn't nearly so settled today as it was in your grandmother's Sunday school class. The truth about the matter certainly hasn't changed. Truth is eternal and never changes. But what has changed is people's willingness to accept what they have been told about hell simply because somebody they loved or trusted said it.

It is important for you to recognize that this chapter is in no way an attempt to offer a thorough treatment on the topic of hell. Countless volumes have been written on the subject over the years, and there is much material available to study if you are interested in digging deeply into the matter. I'm not seeking here to offer you a dogmatic position on the meaning of hell. I'm simply sharing a viewpoint to show you that there are ways to understand hell within the concept of a God who is always loving and not angry.

Can we believe hell exists *and* embrace the reality of a God who isn't angry and who can never do anything less than to love? Yes, we can. Many people have held this perspective since the early days of the church, especially in the Eastern world of Christianity.

While there are those who suggest that hell doesn't even exist, others contend that hell is simply a psychological state of spiritual barrenness and emotional bankruptcy that we experience right now. Most traditional churchgoers argue either from the position of infernalism or of annihilationism. Infernalists insist that unbelievers will suffer unending, conscious torment in a literal fire. Annihilationists believe that unbelievers will eventually be annihilated and simply cease to exist.

My purpose in this chapter isn't to resolve all kinds of questions about hell. If they haven't been settled in 2000 years of discussion and debate, I'm highly unlikely to provide the definitive answers here. Rather, I hope to show you that the subject of hell can and must stand inside a biblical understanding of the love of God. We can fully believe in the love of God without rejecting the whole idea of hell.

A Place and a Condition

"The word *hell* isn't even in the Bible!" Nigel said to me one day, revealing that he didn't believe in hell at all.

"Of course it isn't, Nigel," I answered. "*Hell* is an English word, and the Bible was written in Hebrew and Greek."

Of course, he meant that there is no teaching about hell in the Scriptures. I understand why people might believe that. They think the translations of the Greek words rendered *hell* in English Bibles are always wrong. I don't agree. It is true that in some instances, Bible translators would have done better to translate the Greek word *hades* or the Hebrew word *sheol* as *grave*. And yes, the word *gehenna*, usually translated as *hell*, refers to a garbage dump outside the city of Jerusalem. However, it is important to recognize that those temporal locations are metaphors for eternal realities.

Hell is both a place and a condition. It is a place in the sense that we all continue to live after our bodies have died. Our consciousness, the awareness that we possess at this very moment, doesn't die. We don't simply lapse into a state of nonbeing the instant we breathe our last breath. Like those who believe in Christ, those who want nothing to do with Him still have consciousness and must live somewhere. They still exist, so what is the place in which they exist? Unless you agree with some Universalists, who believe that everybody immediately opens their eyes in the eternal bliss of heaven, the most accurate word that can be used is *hell*. Hold on to that thought though, because shortly I'll tell you that hell might not be as far from heaven as you may think.

Hell is also a condition, and that will be the focus of this chapter. People are sometimes so deeply committed to their current understanding of the nature of hell that if somebody comes along with a different viewpoint, they immediately freak out and accuse anyone holding a different view of not believing in hell at all. I believe in the reality of hell, but in recent years, my view of the nature of hell has changed. I hope that, after considering the evidence presented in this chapter, yours may too.

"If God is love, there can be no such thing as hell," somebody recently posted on Facebook. Immediately, others chimed in that to believe in a God of love who not only created hell but actually sustains it would be a contradiction. But accusing God of saying, "I love you, but if you don't love me back, I'll burn you forever in hell" is a shameful caricature of what those who believe in the existence of hell truly believe. There is a God who is pure love and there is also a real hell.

Are these two ideas mutually exclusive? How can hell be real if God really is pure love? How could He even allow such a thing? How can one argue that God isn't an angry God, as I do in this book, if hell is real? How do the two fit together? To answer that question, let's consider several common misconceptions about hell.

Is Hell Outside of God?

The most prevalent teaching about hell is that it is a place where God is absent. In this view, He has cast people into a punishing fire, shut the prison door, and walked away, resolved to never return. However, when we lay that viewpoint alongside what the Bible actually teaches about the pervasive presence of God in His creation, the position quickly withers. Here is what the apostle Paul had to say about God's presence in all of creation: "The Son is the image of the invisible God, the firstborn over all creation. For in him all things were created: things in heaven and on earth, visible and invisible, whether thrones or powers or rulers or authorities; all things have been created by him and for him. He is before all things, and *in him all things hold together*" (Colossians 1:15-17 NIV).

Nothing exists that is not created and sustained by the Creator. If the One who holds everything together were to be absent from any place, that place would instantly cease to exist. Hell, then, is not the absence of God. God is not absent from anything, but is in the immediate presence of everything. If God is omnipresent, He cannot be absent from hell. You can't have it both ways. The fact is, our God is everywhere at every moment.

Certainty and Pride

Changing our perspective on a truth like this doesn't come easily if our belief system is set like concrete. When we are absolutely, positively sure that our viewpoint is the correct view—when we refuse to consider that there may be another way of seeing it—the Holy Spirit must work a miracle to teach us something new. When we are convinced that our view is the only viable way to understand the matter and we summarily dismiss anything different as being wrong, change doesn't come without resistance.

Prideful certainty about things that sincere Bible students have long debated affects us more than we may know. I'm not talking here about nonnegotiable foundations of our faith that have defined Christianity from the beginning. I'm referring to controversial topics that have been debated through church history by serious students of the Bible.

With topics like these, we need not insist that our viewpoint is the only one that could possibly be correct.

Historically, the subject of hell has never been considered a fundamental tenet of the Christian faith. That has changed over the past few years in some parts of the church. Nowadays, if your view of hell is different from others', you'd better be prepared to be called a heretic. But as you consider this subject, remember that church leaders have always had different opinions about the nature of hell. If we are close-minded about this subject, we don't honor Christ, and we are actually being shallow in our pursuit of biblical truth. We aren't guilty of compromising simply because we take another look at what the Bible says to check our beliefs.

This closed mindset is pervasive with many about various areas of biblical truth today. Remember, when we discuss hell, we aren't weakening a plank in the theological platform of salvation. We are simply discussing the nature of hell. Nonetheless, some folks get as mad as you can imagine about the subject. Allow me to give you an example with Hilary, a high-spirited opponent of my teaching about hell.

The Presence of God

Hilary got right up in my face one day, and in a tone that was almost a little frightening, she said to me, "You say you believe the Bible, but you really don't!"

"Why do you say that?" I asked her in a lower volume, hoping to deflate the tension in the air.

"Because of what you said about hell. God is not present in hell, and I can prove it to you from the Bible," she said.

"Okay, let's talk about it," I responded. "What part of the Bible do you have in mind?"

She opened her Bible to a place she had bookmarked. Pointing to the verse, she read 2 Thessalonians 1:9 to me, over-enunciating every word. "These will pay the penalty of eternal destruction, away from the presence of the Lord and from the glory of His power." She tapped the phrase "away from the presence of the Lord" with her index finger as she read it. "Do you believe what that says?" she asked.

"Yes, of course I believe what it says," I answered, "but can we talk about what it means?"

"It means what it says!" she answered.

"Okay," I answered. "Then let's see where it says that in other places in the Bible too. Then we'll compare to see what it actually means when it *says* that these will be 'away from the presence of the Lord.'"

"What do you think it means?" she asked with obvious cynicism.

"Well, let's look at a few other verses, and then I'll let you decide what the phrase means," I answered. "In Genesis 4:16, the Bible says, 'Then Cain went out from the presence of the LORD, and settled in the land of Nod, east of Eden.' Then there's the story of Jonah running from God. Jonah 1:3 says he boarded a boat to go 'to Tarshish from the presence of the LORD.'

"Let's just stop for now with those two verses," I said to Hilary. "Look at the way the phrase 'from the presence of the LORD' was used. Did Cain really leave the presence of God when he went to the land of Nod? Was God not there? Or when Jonah fled from the presence of the Lord, did God not go with him? You see, the phrase 'away from the presence of the LORD' doesn't mean that God isn't there. It refers to a place of rebellion where people can't experience God's loving blessings because of their attitude, not His. What do you think the phrase means in those verses?"

"Well, there are other places in the Bible that show unbelievers are alone without God in hell," Hilary answered, ignoring my question.

I knew there was no need in continuing the discussion. Hilary wasn't open to learning something. She only wanted to set me straight.

Seeing What We Want to See

Do you see the point I was making with her? This verse in 2 Thessalonians 1:9 is just one example of how we can read our preconceived ideas into the Bible. We sometimes see a specific meaning in a passage, but with even a minimum amount of study, we would discover it isn't actually there.

However, since the focus of this chapter is the subject of hell, let's move forward with that discussion. I paused here with this illustration to show how easily our underlying assumptions and understandings can lead us to misinterpret a biblical text. Seeing our vulnerability, let's all resolve to be open to new understandings. We certainly aren't to be gullible, but we do want to be teachable.

We all tend to focus on verses that support our existing viewpoint, but we breeze over passages that might challenge our current understanding. For instance, Hilary's proof text for her view was 2 Thessalonians 1:9. It seemed to say exactly what she already believed, but what of verses like Revelation 14:9-10?

> If anyone worships the beast and its image and receives its mark on their forehead or on their hand, they, too, will drink the wine of God's fury, which has been poured full strength into the cup of his wrath. They will be tormented with burning sulfur *in the presence of the holy angels and of the Lamb* (NIV).

Many people, like Hilary, cling to one understanding of some verses without really noticing other verses that seem to contradict their interpretation. We can't prove our viewpoint by seeing who can create the biggest pile of handpicked Bible verses. We must study the whole counsel of Scripture to avoid distorting doctrines one way or the other.

The idea that God is absent from hell is popular, and people like Hilary can even show you verses that allegedly prove it. But when we study a topic, we need to be humble and teachable instead of stubbornly refusing to consider another way of understanding it. If our current viewpoint is true, can't it withstand scrutiny and honest questions? Hilary evidently didn't think so and was totally unwilling to consider a new perspective.

The Fire of Hell

Some have renounced the idea of hell's existence because they have concluded that their only options are to either believe in the kind of hell they were taught exists or else completely reject it. Fortunately, those are not the only options.

The word that is used most frequently to describe hell is *fire*. The

New Testament repeatedly uses it in connection with judgment. But what exactly is this fire? Is it an expression of eternal anger from God, who has finally reached the end of His grace? Is it contemptuous rage toward those who refused to love Him after He had loved them?

Considering that this same God admonishes us, "Love your enemies, bless them that curse you, do good to them that hate you" (Matthew 5:44 KJV), does it make sense that He would do just the opposite? Does He call on us to behave more nobly toward those who oppose us than He does? Would He call us to live by a higher standard than He lives by? "God is love," says 1 John 4:8. The apostle Paul wrote that love "is not provoked, does not take into account a wrong suffered" (1 Corinthians 13:5). Is that true of God, who *is* love? Or does this biblical description of love apply to everybody else but not to Him? The Scripture assures us that "God was reconciling the world to himself in Christ, not counting people's sins against them" (2 Corinthians 5:19 NIV). Since He doesn't count people's sins against them, what would be the cause for this divine rage that some people imagine?

How, then, do we reconcile the fire of hell with a God whose nature is love? In the proper context, it can be done. Consider this verse in Hebrews 12:29: "Our God *is* a consuming fire." God is fire. God is love. Therefore, that fire is love. The logic is clear. Would your view of hell change if the fire were actually the experience of those in eternity who still loathe God as they are engulfed in the flames of divine love?

Torment and Love

"But hell is a place of torment!" Ned protested after hearing me explain this concept of hell.

"You're right," I answered. "But what if the torment experienced by those who still despise God is actually the inescapable presence of His love? What does our love for our enemies seem like to them?" "'But if your enemy is hungry, feed him, and if he is thirsty, give him a drink; for in so doing you will heap burning coals on his head.' Do not be overcome by evil, but overcome evil with good" (Romans 12:20-21).

Loving actions toward an enemy feel like burning coals heaped onto his head. Is that due to the lover's ill will? No, but it will be the experience of the recipient if that love is loathsome to him. "Overcome evil with good," Paul said. If God clearly wants us to behave that way toward our enemies, it makes no sense to suggest, "He doesn't take that approach at all. No, His response is the complete opposite. You are never to stop loving your enemies, but one day He will stop loving His, and when He does, He is going to pour out contemptuous hatred on them."

"But He is God! You can't judge His actions!" Ned persisted.

"But I can fairly ask whether God is asking me to be more loving than He is, can't I?" I responded. "And if He is, where am I supposed to find this love?"

"So you believe it's just a river of love people will be in?" Ned asked. "Hell for them is to swim in a never-ending *p-o-o-o-l* of love?" he continued, drawing out the word.

Ned's belligerent response is common among those who are unwilling to reconsider a viewpoint they have held for a long time. That kind of resistance is often based in fear. After all, if we're wrong about something we've been so convinced about, what else might we be wrong about? No doubt about it, ironclad viewpoints provide a sense of security, but what if those viewpoints are erroneous? Don't we want to know the truth?

Could the love of God really be the fire that torments those who reject Him? Are we going overboard to suggest that His love may be experienced as fire? Let's see what Scripture suggests. Exodus 24:16-18 describes Moses's meeting with God on Mount Sinai.

> The glory of the LORD rested on Mount Sinai, and the cloud covered it for six days; and on the seventh day He called to Moses from the midst of the cloud. And to the eyes of the sons of Israel the appearance of the glory of the LORD was like a consuming fire on the mountain top. Moses entered the midst of the cloud as he went up to the mountain; and Moses was on the mountain forty days and forty nights.

Moses walked into a cloud of God's glory, a cloud of pure love. From down below, Israel looked up and saw him walking into a consuming fire. To Moses it was heaven, but to the rebellious Jews it looked like hell.

Now consider Isaiah 33:10-16.

> "Now I will arise," says the LORD,
> "Now I will be exalted, now I will be lifted up.
> You have conceived chaff, you will give birth to stubble;
> My breath will consume you like a fire.
> The peoples will be burned to lime,
> Like cut thorns which are burned in the fire.
> You who are far away, hear what I have done;
> And you who are near, acknowledge My might."
> Sinners in Zion are terrified;
> Trembling has seized the godless.
> "Who among us can live with the consuming fire?
> Who among us can live with continual burning?"
> He who walks righteously and speaks with sincerity,
> He who rejects unjust gain
> And shakes his hands so that they hold no bribe;
> He who stops his ears from hearing about bloodshed
> And shuts his eyes from looking upon evil;
> He will dwell on the heights,
> His refuge will be the impregnable rock;
> His bread will be given him,
> His water will be sure.

What does Isaiah say about this fire? He says that some will experience it like cut thorns being burned. The description is indeed fearful. Sinners in Zion are terrified, and trembling has seized the godless. The best possible word to describe their plight is *hell*.

However, others who experience that same fire relate to it quite differently. The sinners ask, "Who among us can live with the consuming fire? Who among us can live with continual burning?" Isaiah answers, "He who walks righteously and speaks with sincerity, he who rejects unjust gain…and shuts his eyes from looking upon evil."

Sinners and saints experience the same fire. The first group would be terrified, but the latter group had nothing to fear. It doesn't scare them at all.

Eternity Doesn't Have Zip Codes

Earlier I mentioned that hell might not be as far from heaven as you think. Where is this river of fire that brings such terror to some? Daniel 7:10 gives us the answer.

> A river of fire was flowing,
>   coming out from before him.
> Thousands upon thousands attended him;
>   ten thousand times ten thousand stood before him (NIV).

Daniel saw God, the Ancient of Days, sitting on His throne, which itself was ablaze with flames (verse 9). From that flaming throne flowed a river. In Daniel's vision, everyone is there in the presence of this river and the One from whom it flows. There are no subdivisions in the eternal realm. In Daniel's vision, everybody is in the same place. Once we leave the temporal, the only place we can be is in the eternal. And in that eternal realm, we all will meet God face-to-face. When we do, we will see a river of flames gushing from His fiery throne.

What is this river of fire? It is the raging torrent of divine agape, and everybody is present. A large group ministers to Him, and an even larger group stands by, but everybody is there in the presence of this burning love. It will be heaven to some and hell to others, depending on how they relate to God's love. Some receive His love and others reject it, but He loves nonetheless. What else is He who *is* love to do?

Thomas Merton offered this explanation.

> Our God is a consuming fire. And if we, by love, become transformed into Him and burn as He burns, his fire will be our everlasting joy. But if we refuse His love and remain in the coldness of sin and opposition to Him and to other men then will His fire (by our choice rather than His) become our everlasting enemy, and Love, instead of being our joy, will become our torment and our destruction.[2]

An Interpretation with Deep Roots

If you have spent your life in the Western Evangelical church, this understanding of hell may create a sort of shell shock for you because it is so new and so different from what you've always been taught and believed. But the viewpoint I'm suggesting here isn't new at all. It has its roots in the Bible and was taught by the early church. In some parts of the world, this is the only view of hell Christians have ever held, and they scratch their heads in puzzlement that Western believers could see it in the way we typically do.

> The Eastern Church has long regarded hell subjectively, as an existential experience. But rather than a question of inclusion and exclusion, they conceive of heaven and/ or hell as two experiences of the same fire. To their way of thinking, God is the fire that we experience as either a blessing or a torment, depending on our spiritual state.[3]

Seventh-century theologian and bishop Isaac the Assyrian held the same view.

> I say, that those who are suffering in hell, are suffering in being scourged by love…It is totally false to think that the sinners in hell are deprived of God's love. Love is a child of the knowledge of truth, and is unquestionably given commonly to all. But love's power acts in two ways: it torments sinners, while at the same time it delights those who have lived in accord with it.[4]

Born in Thessaloniki, Greece, in 1931, theologian Alexandre Kalomiros came to Seattle, Washington, in 1980 to give a series of talks called "The River of Fire." The talks contrast Eastern church and Western church teachings on various biblical subjects. His talks were so widely received that they later were published in writing under the same title. On the subject of hell, he offered this explanation.

> The Light of Truth, God's Energy, God's grace which will fall on men unhindered by corrupt conditions in the Day of

Judgment, will be the same to all men. There will be no distinction whatever. All the difference lies in those who receive, not in Him Who gives. The sun shines on healthy and diseased eyes alike, without any distinction. Healthy eyes enjoy light and because of it see clearly the beauty which surrounds them. Diseased eyes feel pain; they hurt, suffer, and want to hide from this same light which brings such great happiness to those who have healthy eyes...

The very fire which purifies gold, also consumes wood. Precious metals shine in it like the sun, rubbish burns with black smoke. All are in the same fire of Love. Some shine and others become black and dark. In the same furnace steel shines like the sun, whereas clay turns dark and is hardened like stone.

The difference is in man, not in God.[5]

The difference, then, is in how the individual relates to divine love. It is not a matter of God's loving acceptance of those who have believed and scornful rejection of those who haven't. Our God's nature doesn't change because one day the grace clock finally runs down. "I am the LORD, and I do not change," He once told rebellious Israel (Malachi 3:6 NLT). If God is a God of loving grace now, and He is, then we have His guarantee that He won't change at some point in the future.

Can you see how hell isn't a contradiction of the love of God? Those who have rejected the idea of the very existence of hell have actually rejected the popular pseudo-hell that they have heard about. It's the one where Divine Love's love finally ends and it's time to pay the piper. It's the one where Grace acts ungraciously by walking away in disgust. It's the one where the very DNA of the Trinity mutates, and God carries out a hell-bent vendetta regardless of how many are hurt or destroyed in the process. It is the hell of Dante, with nine narrowing cells of increasing torment inflicted by executive order of a Cosmic Warden who expresses no compassion toward the incarcerated. It is the hell designed by One who may have been kind for a while, but that day is over now. *That* hell needs to be rejected. Count me among those who reject it.

Some people will experience hell, not because God is angry with them, but because they have chosen it. C.S. Lewis wrote, "There are only two kinds of people in the end: those who say to God, 'Thy will be done,' and those to whom God says, in the end, 'Thy will be done.' All that are in Hell, choose it."[6] Damnable pride is an addictive, intoxicating, and ultimately catastrophic possession that some will go to hell to keep from forfeiting.

Is There Any Chance Later?

With the idea in mind that God's grace truly is eternal, the question logically surfaces, will some people leave hell by repenting in the afterlife? Oddly, I've found that the answer I offer typically stirs up a greater reaction than if I were to say yes, people most definitely will come out of hell in the next world. My answer is, I don't know. That answer galls some people, as if those who write books and teach at Bible conferences ought to know.

In fact, many Evangelicals are convinced they do know and think that to even raise the question as I have done is deplorable if not outright heretical. At the least they would accuse one who considers such a question to be toying with the Roman Catholic idea of purgatory. The charge is understandable because of the suggestion that there may be an opportunity to experience grace in the next world. This section, however, has nothing to do with the doctrine of purgatory.

In Catholic doctrine, purgatory is a place of purification based on the Roman church's viewpoint that "nothing unclean will enter the presence of God in heaven and, while we may die with our mortal sins forgiven, there can still be many impurities in us, specifically venial sins and the temporal punishment due to sins already forgiven."[7] We have already established that no place exists where God is not present. To the contrary, the Catholic viewpoint concerning purgatory is that "nothing unclean will enter the presence of God." So the position of the Roman Catholic Church suggests that some people are separated from God's presence in the afterlife. I have plainly stated that nothing and nobody is separated from God. The contradiction between these two clearly shows that what I am presenting here is not purgatory. Those who think otherwise simply can't find the proper mental folder to file this information in, so they file it under purgatory.

Not Knowing Is Okay

Evangelicals are generally resolute in their understanding of the details about hell. As a result of that certitude, they consider others of us—who are comfortable with more biblical ambiguity and who embrace a greater level of mystery—as simply being afraid to admit what we really believe. I've been falsely accused more than once of being afraid to admit publicly what I really believe. If that were true, I certainly would not write a book like this. Religious zealots throughout church history have martyred people for saying less than I have written in this book.

No, the simple fact is that we cannot be dogmatic about some things, based on what the Bible says. As author Brad Jersak says, it's not that the Bible says too little about some subjects. To the contrary, on some things it seems to say too much, leaving us to grapple with paradoxical statements that we can't quite reconcile. Most people choose one side or the other when they encounter tension on a subject the Bible addresses. Many people can't abide the position of not knowing.

Despite Evangelicals' almost universal demand for complete certitude and resistance to mystery, it is perfectly acceptable to say we don't know. Many believers would greatly benefit from learning to confess that simple statement from the heart, and the church at large would be a lot better off as a result.

One thing the Bible is certainly not ambiguous about is the duration of God's mercy. Psalm 136 affirms 26 times in 26 verses, "For His mercy endures forever" (NKJV). That's just one chapter in the Old Testament—the tip of the iceberg. It stands to reason that eternal grace would offer eternal mercy. Does God's grace finally expire at some point, or does it last forever? How can we suggest that divine mercy will end if we truly believe that His very nature is one of grace? Surely, we will never see a day when He morphs into a different kind of God than He has revealed Himself to be in Jesus. He isn't a God of temporary grace, nor is He a God of partial grace. Remember, He never changes.

Grace isn't just an approach He takes toward us. It is an expression of who He is!

On one hand, there is enough biblical evidence to warrant raising the question about possibilities in the afterlife. But on the other, there isn't enough to make an affirmative claim with ironclad certainty. Is there any chance in the afterlife for those who didn't believe on Christ during this lifetime? That isn't a heretical question to ask, although those who are convinced they already have definitive answers on such matters usually scorn such questions. There is no such thing as a heretical question. There are only heretical answers.

This Isn't New Either

To leave the question about hope after death lying unanswered in the arms of Mystery incites an immediate reaction from Universalists, who are persuaded that everybody will one day believe on Jesus and be in heaven. It also usually provokes outrage among those who hold the more typical Evangelical position on the matter. My goal here isn't to persuade you to take either position, but in fairness to the subject, we do well to note that many throughout church history have held such a hope for those who died without professing faith in Christ in this life.

Consider Martin Luther, the revered hero of almost all informed Protestants. The mention of his name brings a mental thumbs-up among most Protestant churchgoers. What was his viewpoint on this question? In a letter to a friend he wrote, "God forbid that I should limit the time of acquiring faith to the present life. In the depth of the Divine mercy there may be opportunity to win it in the future."[8] We don't hear about that much, do we? Why not? It's because the contemporary culture of the Evangelical church doesn't like questioning that sort of thing and likes Luther's answer even less. How far would Luther, the prominent Reformer who gave rise to Protestantism, get saying that kind of thing in the Protestant church today? Not far, I suspect.

We can easily go further back into church history to demonstrate the presence of hope about hell. For instance, here's what Clement of Alexandria, a prominent theological voice of the late second and early third century, had to say: "We can set no limits to the agency of the

Redeemer to redeem, to rescue, to discipline in his work, and so will he continue to operate after this life."[9] I don't see Pastor Clement getting a warm welcome if he wanted to preach that in the corner church in my neighborhood, do you? He would be bounced out on his head among most twenty-first-century denominations.

Even Augustine, the champion of eternal torment, wrote early in the fifth century, "There are very many who though not denying the Holy Scriptures, do not believe in endless torments."[10] Augustine believed that the many who held a different view from his weren't denying the Holy Scriptures in their beliefs. Many Christians today aren't so charitable in their assessment of dissenters.

Many others throughout church history have embraced what German theologian Jürgen Moltmann called a "theology of hope." Those who would immediately dismiss the hope that many have had for those who leave this world without trusting Christ as being ridiculous would do well to study church history and take another look at the subject in the Bible before harshly condemning it.

The Bible says that our God "desires all men to be saved and to come to the knowledge of the truth" (1 Timothy 2:4). He is a God who is "not wanting anyone to perish, but everyone to come to repentance" (2 Peter 3:9 NIV). It might be wise to use caution before condemning those who hold the same hope as their Father.

Hope Is Just That

On the other hand, there is a big difference between hope and dogma. The Bible provides enough information on the subject to warrant hope, but it doesn't describe the final destiny for every single individual with such clarity that we have no room for reasonable doubt or discussion. Like it or not, the last chapter of the Bible leaves the matter open-ended. The last few verses of the Bible leave us with a cliffhanger.

> Outside are the dogs and the sorcerers and the immoral persons and the murderers and the idolaters, and everyone who loves and practices lying.
>   "I, Jesus, have sent My angel to testify to you these things

for the churches. I am the root and the descendant of David, the bright morning star."

The Spirit and the bride say, "Come." And let the one who hears say, "Come." And let the one who is thirsty come; let the one who wishes take the water of life without cost (Revelation 22:15-17).

The Bible ends with the bride inside the gates and with unbelievers outside the gates. The Sprit and the bride look to those on the outside and say, "Come! If you're thirsty, come! If you want the water of life, it's free! Come! Come! Come!"

Do they come? *The Bible does not answer that question.* We would be presumptuous to argue that they do come in repentance and faith. We can hope. Using deductive reasoning based on other texts and on what we know about our Father's power and goodness, we can draw conclusions based on eager anticipation. But our assumptions cannot bridge the gap between what the Bible says and the final outcome for every individual. We can only go as far as the Bible takes us. We can walk to the edge of the light and stare into the fog before us with great anticipation and hope, but we can't see what we can't see. And we certainly shouldn't construct a dogma based on assumption, regardless of how logical it may seem to us.

Universalists have turned biblical hope into dogmatic assertion. To go that far is to move beyond what is warranted by Scripture. On the other hand, to refuse to hope is to ignore all the biblical texts that Universalists rightly point toward to proclaim our triune God's goodness.

I myself have been falsely called a Universalist at times because of my views. Some (but not all) who have brought this charge against me have done so with an inflammatory sense of urgency and with impassioned emotion that might sway those who haven't studied the topics for themselves. Hope is just that—hope. It is not doctrinal dogma. I do not ascribe to the Universalist position because I feel it requires an unwarranted and presumptuous step from what the Bible plainly says.

Thomas F. Torrance was one of the twentieth century's most influential voices when it comes to an ultimate hope for humanity. In the

1940s, Torrance held an interesting dialogue and debate with renowned New Testament scholar J.A.T. Robinson. The following quote from Torrance was a rebuttal to Robinson's compelling defense of the Universalist viewpoint (that everybody ultimately ends up in heaven).

> All that Dr. Robinson's argument succeeds in doing is to point to the *possibility* that all might be saved in as much as God loves all to the utmost, but it does not and cannot carry as a corollary the *impossibility* of being eternally lost. The fallacy of every Universalist argument lies not in proving the love of God to be universal and omnipotent but in laying down the impossibility of ultimate damnation. Dr. Robinson has cited passages from the New Testament which would seem to him to point in the direction of Universalism, but what of those many other passages which declare in no uncertain terms that at the last judgment there will be a final division between the children of light and the children of darkness? What of the shuddering horror of the words: "It were better for that man had he never been born," which came from the lips of Omnipotent Love? There is not a shred of Biblical witness that can be adduced to support the impossibility of ultimate damnation. All the weight of Biblical teaching is on the other side.[11]

The Bible teaches that in Christ, our triune God has adopted all of humanity into Himself. This objective reality is factual regardless of whether it ever becomes a person's actual, subjective experience. The gospel is the good news of what our sovereign God has done, not what could be done if a frail human will only let Him. Still, apart from personal faith in Jesus Christ, a person will not inherit the kingdom of God, neither now nor in eternity.

Humility and Unity

Some aspects of the afterlife cannot be known and defended as dogma because of the ambiguity we experience when we try to filter infinite reality through our finite understanding. We can embrace paradoxical statements in Scripture without necessarily reconciling every detail in our own understanding. As loving brothers and sisters, we have no place to vilify those whose understanding is different from our own. We can discuss and debate with passion while maintaining an attitude of loving respect for each other. None of us have perfect understanding of anything, but all see "through a glass, darkly." For that reason, humility *must* frame our discussions. Without that, let's not pretend we understand grace, for our lack of humility betrays us and shows that we still see it only from a distance at best.

None of us have cornered the market on the truth. Sincere Bible students come to different conclusions, each being convinced that the Holy Spirit has taught them through prayerful thought and careful Bible study. To demonize each other over differences is the antithesis of the life in grace we profess. May we each be open to learn and to change so that our souls and actions may increasingly be conformed to the image of the One who unites us all together as one in Him.

Chapter 9

Seeing Through Agape's Eyes

We human beings depend on linear thinking to make logical conclusions. We tend to think that learning is a process of progressively moving from being unenlightened to being enlightened. We don't know something, and then we do, like going from a dark room into a well-lit room. It's a neat and tidy progression, an ascent from ignorance toward knowledge.

But spiritual enlightenment often doesn't work that way—not at all. Sometimes it seems just the opposite. When the Teacher is pulling us forward into truth, we can *feel* as if we're moving from the light into the darkness. It's one of those "His ways aren't our ways" sort of things. But here's what is actually happening in this process—our faulty or shortsighted concepts are being taken away from us to make room for a bigger picture. That can be uncomfortable to say the least.

Consider Moses as an example of how this strange way of God works in human experience. The first time he met God was in the bright light of the burning bush (see Exodus 3:2). The bush that wasn't consumed, the Voice, the supernatural shivers that any man would get when he encountered God in such a stark way…it all seems so clear, so certain, so undeniably God at work.

Later, Moses met God in a pillar of cloud and a pillar of fire (see Exodus 13:21). There it was again—the same fire, but this time there was also a cloud. Shadows and Light—it was still Him but not the consistently burning bright fire Moses saw the first time.

Finally, he meets God at Mount Sinai. There, "the people remained at a distance, while Moses approached the thick darkness where God was" (Exodus 20:21 NIV). Light? What light? Nothing but Darkness now—just the Cloud of Unknowing.

So at least for a while, Moses's encounters with God didn't seem to be moving him further and further into an ever-increasing brightness. His journey took him into the darkness with God. His relationship with Yahweh brought him to the place of not knowing so that he might come to know.

Sneaking into Grace

Moving from the known to the unknown to the Known, from light to darkness to the Light, is integral to the grace walk. If we think we always have to be standing in the bright light of clear understanding, we won't go far. Ironically, the more we come to know, the more we understand how very much we still don't know.

The past years have brought me into a deeper intimacy with my Father than I have ever known, but they haven't been without dark moments. The road I have traveled appears similar to the path along which Moses was led. I used to think I had to have all the answers. Mystery wasn't an option, and certainty on every subject was my goal.

In the spring of 2005 I found myself once again being drawn out into the wilderness, away from the security of my comfortable and well-established theological home. I was like a teen sneaking out of the house at night. I didn't tell people what was privately happening in my personal journey deeper into grace. Many times I studied through the night and into the early morning as I agonized over what I now know to be the continuation of the grace pilgrimage that began for me in

1990. I described my introduction to authentic grace in my first book, *Grace Walk*.[1] It was and still remains an awesome part of my life journey, but I now know it was the starting line, not the finish line.

Fifteen years later I sensed myself being taken further into the depths of God's loving grace. I wasn't afraid that what I was seeing was wrong, but three decidedly self-centered questions haunted me.

1. What would people think if I began to say things in new and different ways?
2. What would my new understanding mean to my ministry?
3. How would it affect my personal and public relationships?

Yes, I know, the questions were all very self-absorbed, and they stemmed from pride and fear. It is a *walk*, and I haven't reached the final destination in understanding yet. I still sometimes ask those sorts of spiritually immature questions, but our patient Father is gracious. He answered those three basic questions with these answers.

1. "It doesn't matter what people think unless you want to do your own thing instead of Mine."
2. "Whose ministry?"
3. "Trust Me with that."

A Mystery to Explore

As I prayerfully studied the Bible and meticulously dissected the witness of numerous contemporary theologians and ancient Church Fathers, I spent thousands of hours of personal study over a span of years. As I was carried forward I saw my thoughts opening like a time-lapse video of a rosebud coming to full bloom. A blossom in thick darkness? Who'd have thought it?

Actually, the brightest light I have ever seen appeared in those moments when I sat quietly in the thick darkness. If you truly want to grow in grace, it is important to remember that having all the answers doesn't necessarily mean we have reached His goal for us. To the contrary, He is more interested in our journey and how we trust, follow, and obey Him along the way. I can't control the direction of my growth, just as the limb on the crepe myrtle outside my window can't direct its growth. And neither can you control your own direction unless you try to force it one way or another—in which case the growth will be both deformed and stunted. It makes much more sense to just entrust ourselves to the One who has been growing trees and people for a long time. Fertilize your heart with sincere prayer, zealous study, and a mind yielded to Him and see what He grows.

I remember struggling with the Scripture and the Spirit early one morning when I first began to examine the possibilities on this topic. I prayed in frustration, "Lord, why didn't You make this easier to understand?" I sensed a gentle word surfacing into my consciousness and answering, "I am not a puzzle to be solved. I am Mystery to be explored."

Therein lies the solution. The flesh insists on definitive answers. The Western world thrives on them. Evangelicals are often addicted to them. But our God transcends our rational minds and stands above supposedly flawless human understanding. He rejects our insistence that we have indisputable answers to every question.

The Rabbit Hole of Grace

What are we to do then? The answer is to grow as He grows us. Here are a few important questions for you to answer. Would you want to know the truth if it turned your existing belief system upside down? Would you want to know if it meant your peers would misunderstand you or even reject you? What if the things He taught you put you out of step with the views of your religious community, which you love? Are you willing to walk into the thick darkness even if others "remained at a distance" from you? Are you willing to reconsider some beliefs you were once certain you understood correctly?

These are integral questions to a life in grace. Your answers will most likely determine how far you go. As Morpheus told Neo in *The Matrix*, "You take the blue pill—the story ends, you wake up in your bed and believe whatever you want to believe. You take the red pill—you stay in Wonderland, and I show you how deep the rabbit hole goes." That could well be the voice of our God speaking to you. This rabbit hole of grace is an endless discovery of the depths of Divine Agape. It isn't a journey for the fainthearted who are satisfied with the superficial platitudes and pat answers of shallow religion. On the other hand, for those who sense the inner stirring to launch out into the deep, it is a journey well worth taking despite its inherent risks to the status quo.

Be careful about asking your God to reveal Himself to you, because He may just do it. When God shows up at our house, He often isn't dressed the way we expected Him to be, and He typically doesn't talk the way we thought He would. Not all those who say they want to know Him understand the implications of what they're saying.

Avoiding Deception

Don't believe the things you have read in this book simply because the words are in print or because somebody you trust or respect has written them or recommended them. Believe them because the words have resonated deep within you, because His Spirit is stirring you with an awakening to the truth you have read here. Believe them because you see their biblical foundations. You may have many questions. You would be the exception if you didn't.

If you move beyond an angry God, if you embrace a view of Him that sees His grace as being *this* big, might you be at risk of being deceived? That's a good thing to ask unless the question is grounded in fear. The word *heresy* is thrown around far too freely and casually these days, but there are indeed heretics out there, and heresy is still something to be avoided. I trust, however, that you have seen enough biblical evidence and enough extrabiblical references from the early church to realize that what I have shared here is nothing less than the biblical and historical gospel given to us 2000 years ago.

Let's avoid being misled by something new, but let's also not be held back from the truth by something old, by the things we already believe. That risk is far greater in the contemporary church than we know. Hearing something taught the same way our whole lives doesn't make it right. Don't mistake familiarity for orthodoxy.

Do the things you have read in this book ring true within you? Sometimes the heart knows before the head catches up with the truth. I still have questions about aspects of God's goodness. I can't harmonize everything I read in the Bible, but I don't have to do that to know the goodness of our triune God's grace. I'm continuously repenting (changing my mind) as I travel along on this grace path, where the light grows brighter as I progress across the valleys of doubts and the hills of discovery. Little did I know in 1990, when it all began, that my grace walk would become an unending grace pilgrimage into the depths of Divine Goodness, exceeding anything I could have imagined then. It just keeps getting better and better! Isn't that just like our God?

"How has your growing view of theology changed you in practical ways?" a friend asked me one day. That was a good question. If theological understanding only rearranges our mental filing cabinet, who cares? In theology, Heavenly Mystery meets human minds, and the result is an outpouring of divine life and love. It is the lens through which we will see God, others, and ourselves. If it doesn't affect us in these areas, it's philosophical candy at best and nutritionless Bible-babble at worst.

A Clearer Understanding of God

Moving beyond the concept of an angry God may be the greatest spiritual need in everybody's life. Albert Einstein indirectly affirmed as much when he said, "I think the most important question facing humanity is, 'Is the universe a friendly place?' This is the first and most basic question all people must answer for themselves."

The answer to his question is found in the nature of the Creator of the whole cosmos. Yes, the universe is a friendly place because it is an expression of the One who spoke it into existence. The essence of *perichoresis* is a friendly disposition. The whole cosmos finds its home in the *perichoretic* union of the Father, Son, and Spirit, so it can be no other way. Adam's whine can't drown out Love Divine.

A friendly God created a friendly world in which He could place His friends to temporarily live. Understanding God's friendly posture toward us changes everything. The external circumstances of life might easily lead us to question the Creator's love for those He created. All of us have faced difficult situations, and we wonder how to reconcile the imminent presence of a loving God with our immediate predicaments. Jesus loves me, this I know, but this hard world won't tell me so!

God's Love Changes Everything

The deep, settled conviction that God is love changes everything. It fits our pain in this natural world into the greater context of the supernatural, eternal world. As we see our problems in that context, we find an internal peace in the midst of external turmoil. Always filter the external through the eternal before allowing it to become internal.

Pain is still pain. Moving beyond an angry God doesn't insulate us from the feelings inherent to living in this world. But it gives us an anchor in the storms of life that supports us by providing a deep sense of peace that everything will be okay—even when we don't know how and when everything we feel suggests just the opposite.

There may be no greater mental and emotional torment than wrestling with accusing questions while you're in the middle of a hellish problem. What did I do wrong? What could I have done differently? Why isn't God doing something to help me right now? Why don't I have more faith? Why won't He answer my prayers? Questions like these crush us like an avalanche when we aren't convinced of God's absolute love for us in every situation.

Have you settled in your own mind on the reality of God's absolute love? Do you still find yourself grappling with whether love is just one of His qualities alongside others? If you want to grow in grace and live in peace, *you must settle the answer to this question.* I pray you won't finish this book without settling it. Until you irrevocably embrace the unequivocal and unchanging love of God, you will find yourself voting on His love every time your circumstances change for the worse.

Taking a Stand

I'm going to pause here to give an old-fashioned gospel invitation— the kind you may have heard growing up in church. Sometimes the old ways are still good ways.

Will you repent of your faulty thinking about God right now? Will you pause in your reading, take a moment, and affirm to Him that you *do* believe that He, by essence, is pure love and that you will stand on that reality from this point forward in life? Go ahead, make your confession of faith right here, right now. Pray it to Him in your own words.

Now *stand on it.* The love of God isn't negotiable, so from this moment forward, don't ever allow yourself to negotiate about it again. It is settled, so keep it settled in your mind. You aren't a victim of your thoughts. You don't have to be driven about by negative feelings and thoughts, so don't ever act as if you're helpless.

You can't decide what thoughts come into your mind, but you can choose what to do with them when they come. Feelings rise, and we have no control over that, but we can refuse to allow feelings to spill over into our thoughts and create a negative, faithless mindset. Feel what you feel. Own it and don't deny it, but confront negative feelings with the truth of God's love. He isn't angry, so refuse to believe otherwise.

Dorothy Bernard, an American actress of the silent era, said that courage is fear that has said its prayers. In that same vein, faith is an urge to doubt that has chosen to believe the truth instead. You aren't helpless when it comes to what you believe. Embrace the truth of God's grace and never move backward into the concept of an angry God again. God has empowered you to stand in the truth, so do it.

Once we have moved beyond an angry God and met Him as He is, we have discovered the single greatest key for navigating the ups and downs of life. No matter what happens, if we know that Love Personified is sovereign over the affairs of life, we will find in Him the tenacity to face any situation.

Seeing Others Through His Eyes

Moving beyond an angry God has also reshaped the way I see others. There was a time when I saw unbelievers as those who stood apart from me, but the fact is, if Jesus showed us anything, He showed us His solidarity with the whole human race. We are united with each other because He has united with us. His incarnation is a testament to having become one of us and one with us.

"Words like Jewish and non-Jewish, religious and irreligious, insider and outsider, uncivilized and uncouth, slave and free, mean nothing. From now on everyone is defined by Christ, everyone is included in Christ." Be careful not to balk at that description. Those aren't my words. They were written by the apostle Paul (Colossians 3:11 MSG).

Don't have a knee-jerk reaction to that verse by mistakenly thinking I'm implying that everybody is a Christian. I'm not suggesting that there is no need for a person to trust in Christ. What I am saying is that everybody is related to God through the finished work of Jesus Christ whether they know it or not. Through the Son and in the ministry of the Spirit, our Father has adopted us. To use the apostle Paul's words, "God decided in advance to adopt us into his own family by bringing us to himself through Jesus Christ. This is what he wanted to do, and it gave him great pleasure" (Ephesians 1:5 NLT). Everybody Jesus died for has been adopted in Him. Everybody. That happened because of what He did, not because of something we might or might not do.

Unbelievers most assuredly need to trust Christ. Apart from that subjective experience, they will always be like the older brother in the story of the prodigal son. They can eternally stand in outer darkness, refusing to enter the eternal party and enjoy what has been their birthright all along. Make no mistake about it, however—the objective reality of what is already theirs by virtue of the Father's relationship to them is real whether they accept it or not. "All that I have *is* [not *can be*] yours," the father told his hardhearted son in Luke 15. Neither the objective nor the subjective side of the cross can be neglected. Both are equally important. It *is* true, and one *must* accept it to benefit from it.

Paul's Example in Athens

Legalistic religion does its best to keep us from seeing others as having already been adopted in Jesus Christ, but the Bible makes the truth known in numerous places. For instance, consider Paul's conversation with the pagans on Mars Hill (see Acts 17). They were worshipping idols and in no way could be considered Christians.

What did Paul tell them when he preached the gospel to them? He told them that he had noticed how devoted they were to their pursuit of religious matters. Then he pointed out one particular idol they worshiped—the one to the unknown god. "Let me tell you about this God you don't know," Paul said as he skillfully began to share the gospel with these Athenian pagans.

"He made everything and everybody," he continued. "He made us so that we would hunger for Him and then be filled by Him, and that is what He wants all of us to experience right now. He's not a far-off god somewhere in the clouds. No, He is near us, here with us in this very moment!"

Then Paul went straight to the heart of the matter. Read carefully these words he preached to unbelieving pagans in Acts 17:28-29: "For in Him we live and move and exist, as even some of your own poets have said, 'For we also are His children.' Being then the children of God, we ought not to think that the Divine Nature is like gold or silver or stone, an image formed by the art and thought of man."

Who is this "we" Paul referred to? Do you think for a moment that when Paul said, "In Him *we* live and move and exist," he pointed to himself and a few fellow-travelers, intentionally excluding the pagans to whom he was preaching? Of course he didn't. He wanted them to know we *all* live and move in God. Then Paul did what would be unthinkable in many churches today. He quoted one of their own pagan poets to make his point. They knew the words well. The fifth line of the pagan poem *Phaenomena* said, "For we are indeed his offspring."[2]

Study that text carefully. Don't let your mind immediately rush to other verses that seem to suggest something different before you determine how you are going to understand *this* verse. It's easy to run away from biblical texts that scare us because they say something we haven't believed. We want to run back to the perceived safety of verses that seem to support what we already believe. Please don't do that at this point. "We also are His children," Paul told them all. What will you do with that?

Don't think for a moment that Paul was saying we are all God's creation, because that's not what he said. He used the Greek word *genos*, from which we get the English word *geneaology*. Paul wanted them to know their true identity.

After sharing their identity in Christ with them he went on to say, "Now, since you know we all are children of God, it makes no sense to keep believing that God is an idol made of gold, silver, or stone. So repent (change your mind) and believe in Him and what He has already done for you."

Before the Cross and After

Okay, Les. I could hear you shouting in my thoughts as I wrote those last two paragraphs. I know you're eager to make your point. Go ahead.

"Yeah, Steve. You're forgetting that Jesus told the Pharisees they were of their father, the devil!" (This conversation with Les actually happened after he had watched one of my teachings on my YouTube channel.)

"Do you mean *before* He had brought their eternal adoption to them in this temporal world by His crucifixion on the cross?" I asked him.

Make a note of this next statement because it is big: Everything changed with the death, burial, and resurrection of Jesus! Adam died, and a new race was brought into existence.

That answer didn't satisfy Les, so he continued, "But John 1:12 says, 'But as many as received Him, to them He gave the right to become children of God.'"

"That's right, Les," I answered, "but what does that mean? It means that they became children of God in the same way that I might say to a 40-year-old who continuously behaves irresponsibly, 'Will you accept your responsibilities and become a man?' The fact is, he is already a man. I'm challenging him to receive his manhood and experientially become who he already is biologically."[3]

Les finally began to connect to this truth after numerous discussions. One day he said, "So it's like my dad used to tell me, 'You are a Smith. Now *be* one!'"

Exactly.

No Insiders or Outsiders

> For in God's union with this one man, Jesus Christ, he
> has shown his love to all and his solidarity with all. In this
> One he has taken upon himself the sin and guilt of all, and
> therefore rescued them all by higher right from the judg-
> ment which they had rightly incurred, so that he is really
> the true consolation of all.[4]

The word *all* keeps coming up in the theology of the apostle Paul
and many others who have moved beyond an angry God. *All* means
everybody.

Consider one more example of how understanding humanity's
adoption in Christ changes the way we see people. This biblical narrative challenges the attitude that excludes others today, just as it challenged Peter 2000 years ago.

God had sent Peter to the house of Cornelius to share the gospel
with those there. Cornelius was a Gentile who knew so little theological truth that when Peter arrived at his home, Cornelius fell down to
worship him (see Acts 10:25). This seeker was spiritually zealous but
certainly not well-versed in the truth.

Peter was convinced God had told him to go share the gospel, but
there was a problem. Peter needed to get his mind right first. That usually doesn't come easily to any of us. Repentance sometimes hurts. It's
not easy admitting we've been wrong, especially if we've been wrong
a long time.

Peter was a devout Jew who didn't want to talk with Cornelius, who
was a Gentile. He so resisted visiting with this "outsider," God had to
give him a vision to change his mind so he would be willing to go. In
this vision, Peter saw a sheet descending from heaven with all types of
unclean animals in it. He had a buffet of nonkosher meat set down
right before him, and then he heard God say, "Cook this and eat it."

The very idea of eating unclean meat was disgusting to this devout
Jew, but God had something to teach him, and it wasn't about meat. It
was about people. "There is *no way*, Lord! I have *never* eaten anything
unholy or unclean."

"Don't consider something unholy that I have called clean," God said to him. The Lord had to go through this with Peter three times to get the message across to him (see Acts 10:9-16).

Finally, after repenting of his attitude of excluding people whom God had included, Peter went to Cornelius's house. When he went inside, he told them that he had been unwilling to come but that God had given him a vision. "God has shown me that I should not call any man unholy or unclean," he admitted.

Us Versus Them

Peter had drawn a dividing line between those he imagined to be holy and those who were not. This same "us versus them" division exists in the church today. We see some people as out and some people as in, but the Bible teaches that this view of mankind is inconsistent with what happened as a result of the incarnation of Jesus in this world. May He teach us the same thing He taught Peter.

Some would argue that this text tells us only that Gentiles as well as Jews were now included in the gospel, but that viewpoint limits the gospel of grace. God told Peter not to consider anything unclean that He had called clean. There's the Jewish reference to unclean foods, but God also told Peter not to call anything (or anybody) unholy when He had cleaned it (and them). Don't miss the central message of this story—*inclusion*. The good news is that everybody is included in what Jesus has done on our behalf. Not one people group stands apart from the love of the Father expressed in the finished work of Jesus. We have all been adopted in Him.

That's why Paul, after describing with breathtaking beauty that Christ died for the whole human race and that all died with Him, also wrote, "So we have stopped evaluating others from a human point of view" (2 Corinthians 5:16 NLT).

This is precisely how moving beyond an angry God has transformed the way I see people. I don't see them through the lens of exclusion and judgment but rather through the eyes of loving acceptance. We all were included in what He has done for us in Jesus, as Norman Grubb explains.

And what more perfect and final insight in the right ways of seeing fellow-humans than the Savior's own words on the cross: "Father, forgive them for they know not what they do"? Jesus looked through brutal cruelty or careless indifference to precious humans in ignorance, and doing what they thought to be right, and that is what the Father's forgiveness is for.

Now I apply that to my daily reactions to people. I must not keep my believing, as I have done for so long, on outward appearances. I must not lump together all the people involved in some combined action I disapprove of (and my disapproval of the action may be largely because I don't understand) as just a crowd of prejudiced or self-seeking people; but I must see them as individuals, in each of whose hearts God is working as He is in mine. Equally I must not look with a jaundiced eye on individual outward behavior or appearance of which I don't approve. I must practice this same principle of transferred believing, transferred to who each person really is—a created and loved human in the being of God, *really therefore a form of God, a human expression of God, gone wrong*—that he may be made right; and God in His Spirit of love is as busy working in him, disturbing his false beliefs, as He has been on me through the years. Then I love my neighbor as myself. Just as I always find tolerance for myself, so I can for my neighbor.[5]

Loving people—that's what it's all about in this world. Mankind's inclusion in the finished work of Christ doesn't mean that everybody has received it or is experiencing the benefits of it now or will necessarily experience the benefits of it when they die. The gospel message, however, is that we all *are* included in Him and what He has done on our behalf. Accept it and be blessed. Reject it to your own peril. The work of God in Jesus through the Spirit is what it is.

This gospel we proclaim isn't a message of what can be but is the good news of what already is in Jesus Christ. We don't bring a sales pitch to the unbelieving world. We are ambassadors for Christ, and we tell everybody, "God was in Christ reconciling you to Himself. He does not count your sins against you. You are forgiven, and He has received you. Now, receive Him." These are the two sides to one coin. One side has been settled in eternity, and the other side settles it experientially. One side shows what *has* happened, and the other side shows what *does* happen as a person believes on Him.

Some Universalists will tell you that faith is a work, but that is nonsense. Faith is the joyful acceptance of what is already true. Faith isn't something we *do* but is the spontaneous explosion of an enthusiastic embracing of Jesus and what He has given us in Himself.

Do I believe in the ultimate reconciliation of humanity to God? Oh, no. It's better than that. I believe in the *historical* reconciliation of humanity to our loving Creator, who is also our Father. Without asking for so much as a nod of approval from us, before we were even born or could have an opinion on the matter, while we were yet helpless, sinners, enemies of God—He went and did it all. He took the sins of Adam's race into His human body on a cross and died the death sin brings, and in so doing, we all died with Him. He was buried, taking the sons and daughters of Adam to that dark finality from which we would never return. He rose on the third day, bringing with Him a new race of sons and daughters who possessed a kind of life that had never even existed.

The Living Dead

Are some still dead to that very life they possess? Yes they are. Don't think of that as a contradiction or an oxymoron. Paul once said about widows in the church who were caught up in cheap thrills, "The widow who lives for pleasure is dead even while she lives" (1 Timothy 5:6 NIV). I've never even insinuated in these pages that unbelievers aren't dead. They are, but they are dead to the life they have in Christ. Can a person simultaneously be dead in one sense and alive in another? "Dead even while she lives," Paul said. It would seem so.

Rob Bell showed us all what happens when you paint the picture of God's grace with a broad stroke. Raise too many questions or go further with grace than some do, and there will be a price to pay. Robert

Capon's words have become a banner for all of us who share this view of big grace from a big God. Most of us have quoted him on this point.

> I am and I am not a universalist. I am one if you are talking about what God in Christ has done to save the world. The Lamb of God has not taken away the sins of some—of only the good, or the cooperative, or the select few who can manage to get their act together and die as perfect peaches. He has taken away the sins of the world—of every last being in it—and he has dropped them down the black hole of Jesus' death. On the cross, he has shut up forever on the subject of guilt: "There is therefore now no condemnation…" All human beings, at all times and places, are home free whether they know it or not, feel it or not, believe it or not.
>
> But I am not a universalist if you are talking about what people may do about accepting that happy-go-lucky gift of God's grace.[6]

That plainly says it. What Jesus did affected everybody whether we believe it or not, but we won't experientially profit from what He did without receiving it. God doesn't send anybody in hell to punish them, but there will be hell to pay by those who insist on holding on to their sins and not Him. In Jesus, everybody has been adopted by the Father, but we can still live as children of wrath and children of disobedience if we're that stubborn. We are all rich, filthy rich in Him, but we can live like destitute orphans for all eternity if that's what we'd rather do. We have all been found, but if we want to wander around like lost fools, nobody will stop us.

Christ's objective work is finished regardless of our response. To enjoy it, we respond with subjective belief. Some people become agitated by this teaching, but it's still true.[7] Don't let this book be your only input on these subjects. Study for yourself and come to your own conclusions. This isn't a test to see which author or Bible teacher can give the most convincing argument. We are talking about eternal truth, and you don't need to embrace a secondhand viewpoint. Let this book be the starting line for you, not the finish line. Don't make this a contest in which you either vote this message off the island or give it another day to survive. Instead, study. Pray. Open your mind and your heart, and the Teacher *will* guide you into all truth, just as Jesus promised.

If you step out of the shadows of restricted grace, some people will likely misunderstand you, but the benefits are worth the risk. I'd like to end this book with a quote and an example I used in my first book, *Grace Walk*. The quote is from "The Allegory of the Cave" in Plato's *Republic*. All these years later, I can think of no better description of what happens when we move beyond an angry God into the light of a God of unfathomable grace.

> Imagine a cave, says Socrates, very far underground and with a long passage leading out into the daylight. In this cave there are men who have been prisoners there since they were children. They are chained to the ground, and even their heads are fastened in such a way that they can look only in front of them, at the wall of the cave. Behind the line of prisoners a fire is burning, and between the fire and the prisoners there is a roadway. People walk along this road and talk to one another and carry things with them. The prisoners would see the shadows of those people, shadows thrown by the light of the fire on the cave wall in front of them. And, supposing the cave wall reflected sound, the prisoners would hear sounds coming from the shadows. Since the prisoners cannot turn their heads, the only things they will see and know are shadows; and so they will assume that the shadows are *real things*, for they cannot know anything about the fire and the roadway and the people behind them.
>
> Now, suppose we unchain one of the prisoners, and make him turn around. This will be very frightening and painful for him; the movements of his body will hurt him, and his eyes will be dazzled by the fire. And if we tell him that the things he now sees are more real than the shadows, he will not believe us, and he will want to sit down again and face the wall of the shadows which he understands. Now, suppose we go even further than this, and forcibly drag him out

through the long tunnel into the sunlight. This will be even
more painful and frightening for him; and when he arrives
above the ground he will be blinded by the sun. But slowly,
let us imagine, he will get used to it. At first, he will be able to
look at the stars and the moon at night. Later he will look at
the shadows thrown by the sun and at reflections in pools of
water. Finally, he will be able to see the trees and mountains
in full daylight, and he will recognize that these, not the shadows in the cave, are the *real* things. And when he has become
accustomed to looking around him, he will at last realize that
the light which makes all this possible comes from the sun.[8]

In my book *Grace Walk*, I commented on this passage.

> The cave in this allegory represents one's frame of reference.
> I spent twenty-nine years of my Christian life living in the
> cave of legalism. Then the Holy Spirit lovingly began to
> take away those things that provided a sense of security for
> me—visible results in ministry and a sense of satisfaction
> in my Christian life…In spite of my pain and fear, God
> pulled me away from what was familiar and into the light
> of His grace. After several years, my eyes are still adjusting
> to the resplendent glory of grace.[9]

Twenty years have passed since I wrote those words, and I still
find them to be true today. The journey into grace is always a deepening understanding. It always involves being pulled away from what is
familiar so that we might experience the ever-increasing manifestation
of Divine Light. It almost always involves discomfort in the beginning.
It sometimes even involves the loss of acceptance and validation by others who don't see the light you do.

If I have overstated my Father's love in this book, if there is a dark
side of His character of which I've lost sight, a Judicial Temperament
who will hold me accountable for a distorted proclamation of who He
is and what He wants us to know, an incomplete or polluted aspect of
my understanding and declaration of what I sincerely have come to
believe is the true gospel—if I have become confused, misled, beguiled

or misguided in what I wholeheartedly believe has been a revelation of
the meaning of "the finished work of Jesus Christ," then I will apolo-
gize from the bottom of my heart when I get to heaven.

I will plead that where I have been wrong, I have been sincerely
wrong. Wrong after much Bible study and prayer and soul-searching
and agonizing with the Truth. I will humbly and earnestly ask to be forgiven for exaggerating His goodness and grace. But I do not believe that
will ever happen. My Father's grace will always exceed anything you or
I can imagine. I'm gambling everything on that, and it's a gamble I am
confident I will not regret, not in this life or the next. Let the critics say
what they will. Let the like-minded stand together to share this message. Eternity will render the verdict. Let each be fully persuaded in his
own mind and act on that persuasion with boldness.

I implore you to move beyond an angry God and see Him for the
gracious God that He is. Then share this good news. In fact, if necessary, lay down your life for it because if it's true, it's worth it.

Bibliography

Athanasius. *On the Incarnation*. Los Angeles: Empire Books, 2013.

Barclay, William. *New Testament Words*. Louisville: John Knox Press, 1964.

Barth, Karl. *Christ and Adam: Man and Humanity in Romans 5*. Eugene: Wipf and Stock, 1956.

———. *Church Dogmatics*. Peabody: Hendrickson, 2010.

Capon, Robert Farrar. *Between Noon and Three*. Grand Rapids: Eerdmans, 1996.

———. *Kingdom, Grace, Judgment: Paradox, Outrage, and Vindication in the Parables of Jesus*. Grand Rapids: Eerdmans, 2002.

———. *The Parables of Grace*. Grand Rapids: Eerdmans, 1988.

———. *The Romance of the Word: One Man's Love Affair with Theology*. Grand Rapids: Eerdmans, 1996.

Crowder, John. *Cosmos Reborn: Happy Theology on the New Creation*. Marylhurst: Sons of Thunder Ministries, 2010.

Du Toit, Francois. *God Believes in You*. Hermanus, South Africa: Mirror Word, 2013.

———. *The Mirror Bible: A Selection of Key New Testament Texts Paraphrased from the Greek*. Hermanus, South Africa: Mirror Word, 2014.

Grace Communion International. *Trinitarian Conversations: Interviews with Ten Theologians*. Glendora: Grace Communion International, 2014.

Grubb, Norman. *Who Am I?* Blowing Rock: Zerubbabel Press, 1974.

Hodge, Charles. *Systematic Theology*. Peabody: Hendrickson, 2003.

Hunsinger, George. *Disruptive Grace: Studies in the Theology of Karl Barth*. Grand Rapids: Eerdmans, 2000.

———. *How to Read Karl Barth: The Shape of His Theology*. New York: Oxford University Press, 1991.

Jersak, Bradley. *Her Gates Will Never Be Shut.* Eugene: Wipf & Stock, 2009.

Jersak, Bradley, and Michael Hardin, eds. *Stricken by God? Nonviolent Identification and the Victory of Christ.* Grand Rapids: Eerdmans, 2007.

Kettler, Christian. *The God Who Believes: Faith, Doubt, and the Vicarious Humanity of Christ.* Eugene: Wipf & Stock, 2005.

Kruger, Baxter. *The Great Dance.* Jackson: Perichoresis Press, 2000.

———. *Jesus and the Undoing of Adam.* Jackson: Perichoresis Press, 2011.

———. *The Shack Revisited: There is More Going On Here Than You Dared to Dream.* Jackson: Perichoresis Press, 2012.

Lewis, C.S. *The Complete C.S. Lewis Signature Classics.* New York: HarperCollins, 2007.

———. *George MacDonald: An Anthology.* New York: HarperCollins, 2001.

———. *Mere Christianity.* New York: HarperCollins, 2009.

———. *Prince Caspian: The Return to Narnia.* New York: HarperCollins, 1994.

McVey, Steve. *Grace Walk.* Eugene: Harvest House, 1995.

Marshall, Catherine. *Beyond Ourselves.* Grand Rapids: Fleming H. Revell, 1994.

Merton, Thomas. *New Seeds of Contemplation.* New York: New Directions, 2007.

Moltmann, Jurgen. *The Crucified God: The Cross of Christ as the Foundation and Criticism of Christian Theology.* Minneapolis: Fortress Press, 1993.

———. *Theology of Hope.* Minneapolis: Fortress Press, 1993.

Nee, Watchman. *The Normal Christian Life.* Wheaton: Tyndale, 1997.

Richards, E. Randolph, and Brandon J. O'Brien. *Misreading Scripture with Western Eyes: Removing Cultural Blinders to Better Understand the Bible.* Downers Grove: InterVarsity Press, 2012.

Still, William. *Towards Spiritual Maturity.* Tain, Scotland: Christian Focus, 2010.

Tillich, Paul. *The Shaking of the Foundations.* Eugene: Wipf & Stock Publishers, 2012.

Torrance, Thomas F. *Atonement.* Downers Grove: IVP Academic, 2009.

———. *The Mediation of Christ.* Colorado Springs: Helmers & Howard, 1992.

———. *Reality and Evangelical Theology.* Louisville, Westminster John Knox Press, 1981.

———. *Trinitarian Perspectives: Toward Doctrinal Agreement.* New York: T&T Clark, 2000.

Volf, Miroslav. *Exclusion and Embrace: A Theological Exploration of Identity, Otherness and Reconciliation.* Nashville: Abingdon Press, 2010.

Ware, Kallistos. *The Orthodox Way.* Yonkers: Saint Vladimir's Seminary Press, 1995.

Wright, N.T. *Justification: God's Plan & Paul's Vision.* Downers Grove: IVP Academic, 2009.

———. *Simply Jesus: A New Vision of Who He Was, What He Did and Why He Matters.* New York: HarperOne, 2011.

Young, Wm. Paul. *The Shack.* Newbury Park: Windblown Media, 2008.

A Word from the Author

If *Beyond an Angry God* has encouraged you, I would be happy to hear from you. Our purpose at Grace Walk is to share the liberating message of what it means to be in Christ and have Him live His life through us each day. We share this message by teaching in local settings and through radio, television, the Internet, books, audio-video resources, and mission outreaches.

At the time of this publication, Grace Walk Ministries has offices in the United States, Canada, Mexico, Pakistan, Australia, Argentina, and El Salvador. Our leadership team members are all great communicators and are passionate about sharing the message of our God's loving grace. If you would be interested in having any of our team or me speak to your church or group, please feel free to contact us at the address below.

I also invite you to visit our website, where you can learn more about our mission and how we are carrying it out across the world. On the home page of our website, you can also watch "Grace Walk," a Bible teaching I share each week that remains available online throughout that week. To learn more about the subject matter discussed in *Beyond an Angry God*, I invite you to visit www.beyondanangrygod.com. On that site, you will find much helpful information to guide you in your pursuit to continue to grow in grace and in the knowledge of our loving Father.

Grace Walk Ministries
PO Box 6537
Douglasville, GA 30135
www.gracewalk.org
info@gracewalk.org

I also have many other resources available to help you in your own grace walk, including books, CDs, and DVDs which are available at www.vivifire.com. Vivifire offers not only my materials but also sound, grace-based resources from many other authors and speakers.

May God continue to bless you in your own grace walk as you come to "know Him and the power of His resurrection and the fellowship of His sufferings" (Philippians 3:10).

Notes

Introduction

1. C.S. Lewis, *George MacDonald: An Anthology* (New York: HarperCollins: 2001), p. 205.
2. Robert Capon, *Between Noon and Three* (Grand Rapids: Eerdmans, 1996), pp. 140-42.
3. Karl Barth, "How My Mind Has Changed in This Decade: Part Two," *Christian Century*, July 4-11, 1984, p. 684. Available online at www.religion-online.org/showarticle.asp?title=1401.
4. C.S. Lewis, *Prince Caspian: The Return to Narnia* (New York: HarperCollins, 1994), p. 141.
5. Barth, "How My Mind Has Changed in This Decade."

Chapter 1: Grace Is a Dance

1. *The Book of Common Prayer* (New York: Church Publishing, 2007), pp. 326-27.
2. C.S. Lewis, *Mere Christianity* (New York: HarperCollins, 2009), p. 152.
3. Francois Du Toit, *The Mirror Bible* (Hermanus, South Africa: Mirror Word, 2014).
4. C. Baxter Kruger, *Jesus and the Undoing of Adam* (Jackson: Perichoresis Press, 2001), p. 16.
5. Catherine Marshall, *Beyond Ourselves* (Grand Rapids: Fleming H. Revell, 1994), pp. 42-43.
6. Athanasius, *On the Incarnation*, chap. 3, para. 13. Available online at www.ccel.org/ccel/athanasius/incarnation.iv.html.

Chapter 2: Sin Is a Sour Note

1. C.S. Lewis, *The Lion, the Witch and the Wardrobe* (New York: HarperCollins, 1994), p. 45.
2. Athanasius, *On the Incarnation*, chap. 2, para. 6. Available online at www.ccel.org/ccel/athanasius/incarnation.iii.html.
3. Paul Tillich, "You Are Accepted," chap. 19 in *The Shaking of the Foundations* (Eugene: Wipf & Stock, 2012), p. 163. Available online at www.religion-online.org/showchapter.asp?title=378&C=84.
4. Robert Capon, *Between Noon and Three* (San Francisco: Harper & Row, 1982), p. 5.

Chapter 3: Jesus Lived as Us

1. Athanasius, *On the Incarnation*, chap. 3, para. 17. Available online at www.ccel.org/ccel/athanasius/incarnation.iv.html.

2. Thomas F. Torrance, *Trinitarian Perspectives: Toward Doctrinal Agreement* (New York: T&T Clark, 2000), p. 2.

3. Thomas F. Torrance, *The Mediation of Christ* (Colorado Springs: Helmers & Howard, 1992), p. 94.

4. Christian Kettler, *The God Who Believes: Faith, Doubt, and the Vicarious Humanity of Christ* (Eugene: Wipf & Stock, 2005), p. 6.

5. The Heidelberg Catechism is available online at www.ccel.org/creeds/heidelberg-cat.html.

6. Robert Capon, *Between Noon and Three* (Grand Rapids: Eerdmans, 1997), p. 291.

7. Cited in Ned B. Stonehouse, *J. Gresham Machen: A Biographical Memoir* (Carlisle: Banner of Truth, 1977), p. 508.

8. C. Baxter Kruger, *The Great Dance* (Jackson: Perichoresis Press, 2000), p 48.

9. Thomas F. Torrance, *Reality and Evangelical Theology* (Louisville: Westminster John Knox Press, 1981), pp. 14-15.

Chapter 4: Grace Isn't Fair

1. E. Randolph Richards and Brandon J. O'Brien, *Misreading Scripture with Western Eyes: Removing Cultural Blinders to Better Understand the Bible* (Downers Grove: IVP, 2012), p. 11.

2. Walter A. Bordenn, "A History of Justice: Origins of Law and Psychiatry," APPL Newsletter, vol. 24, no. 2, April 1999. Available online at www.aapl.org/newsletter/N242hist_justice.htm.

3. Bradley Jersak and Michael Harden, eds., *Stricken by God? Nonviolent Identification and the Victory of Christ* (Grand Rapids: Eerdmans, 2007), p. 30.

4. Robert Farrar Capon, *Between Noon and Three* (Grand Rapids: Eerdmans, 1997), p. 4.

5. Robert Farrar Capon, *Kingdom, Grace, Judgment: Paradox, Outrage, and Vindication in the Parables of Jesus* (Grand Rapids: Eerdmans, 2002), p. 394.

6. Robert Farrar Capon, *The Parables of Grace* (Grand Rapids: Eerdmans, 1988), p. 141.

7. Kallistos Ware, *The Orthodox Way* (Yonkers: Saint Vladimir's Seminary Press, 1995), pp. 14-15.

8. Cited in Ware, *The Orthodox Way*, p. 25.

9. Charles Hodge, *Systematic Theology* (Peabody: Hendrickson, 2003), p. 446.

Chapter 5: Jesus Wasn't Forsaken

1. E. Randolph Richards and Brandon J. O'Brien, *Misreading Scripture with Western Eyes: Removing Cultural Blinders to Better Understand the Bible* (Downers Grove: IVP, 2012), p. 12.

2. BibleStudyTools.com, www.biblestudytools.com/lexicons/hebrew/nas/nasa.html. I am deeply appreciative to my dear friend Craig Snyder for first introducing me to this wonderful Hebrew word.

3. BibleStudyTools.com, www.biblestudytools.com/lexicons/greek/nas/aphiemi.html.

4. BibleStudyTools.com, www.biblestudytools.com/lexicons/greek/nas/charizomai.html.

Chapter 6: God Isn't Angry

1. BibleStudyTools.com, www.biblestudytools.com/lexicons/greek/nas/hilasterion.html.

2. Anselm, *Cur Deus Homo* [*Why God Became Man*], book 1, chap. 11. Available online at archive.org/stream/curdeushomowhyg00ansegoog#page/n36/mode/2up.

3. Ibid.

4. BibleStudyTools.com, www.biblestudytools.com/lexicons/greek/nas/pas.html.

5. Ibid.

6. Watchman Nee, *The Normal Christian Life* (Wheaton: Tyndale, 1997), p. 38.

7. Thomas F. Torrance, *Atonement* (Downers Grove: IVP Academic, 2009), pp. 188-89.

8. This description comes from the 1998 film adaptation.

9. Norman Grubb, "We Only Know Right Through Wrong," an excerpt from *Who Am I?* (Blowing Rock: Zerubbabel Press, 1974). Available online at www.zerubbabel.org/newsletter/view_article.asp?ID=447&CID=38.

10. BibleStudyTools.com, www.biblestudytools.com/lexicons/greek/nas/thumos.html.

11. BibleStudyTools.com, www.biblestudytools.com/lexicons/greek/nas/orge.html.

12. Ibid.

Chapter 7: His Faith Changed Everything

1. C. Baxter Kruger, *God Is For Us* (Jackson: Perichoresis Press, 1995), p. 41.

2. George Hunsinger *How to Read Karl Barth: The Shape of His Theology* (New York: Oxford University Press, 1991), p. 37.

3. One example of how the translators were inseparably connected to their culture is the way most translations use the word *baptize* in the New Testament. The word isn't actually an English word, but comes from the Greek word *baptizo*, which means, "to dip, to immerse, to submerge." Even the King James translators decided not to translate the word but instead chose to transliterate it (taking Greek letters and converting them to English letters). This was simpler than dealing with the fallout they would have caused by contradicting the practice of sprinkling performed by the Church of England. The point is, we need to compare translations because they all have cultural influences.

4. The genitive construction in Romans 3:26, *ek pisteos Jesou*, is exactly the same in Romans 4:16, where Paul is talking about Abraham's faith—*ek pisteos Abraam*.

5. Irenaeus, *Against Heresies*, book 3, chap. 18, para. 7. Available online at www.ccel.org/ccel/schaff/anf01.ix.iv.xix.html.

6. Athanasius, *On the Incarnation*, chap. 2, para. 9. Available online at www.ccel.org/ccel/athanasius/incarnation.iii.html.

7. William Still, *Towards Spiritual Maturity*, rev. ed. (Tain, Scotland: Christian Focus, 2010), pp. 20-21.

8. William Barclay, *New Testament Words* (Louisville: Westminster John Knox Press, 1964), pp. 167-68. I don't agree with everything written by everybody I quote in this book, but I do agree with the quotes I use. In scholarly books, nobody questions the legitimacy of citing others with whom we disagree on other topics, but in books written for the general population, authors are often guilty by association. This is unwarranted. I would hold many differences with William Barclay, but this assessment of the atonement is stellar.

9. Karl Barth, *Christ and Adam: Man and Humanity in Romans 5*, tr. T.A. Smail (New York: Collier Books, 1962), p. 34.

10. The word *reconciled* in Romans 5:10 is in the aorist tense, indicating a completed event in the past, and the passive voice indicates that it occurred as the result of a force independent of the subject.

Chapter 8: Not Your Grandmother's Hell

1. Robert Capon, *The Romance of the Word: One Man's Love Affair with Theology* (Grand Rapids: Eerdmans, 1996), pp. 9-10.

2. Thomas Merton, *New Seeds of Contemplation* (New York: New Directions, 2007), pp. 123-24.

3. Bradley Jersak, *Her Gates Will Never Be Shut* (Eugene: Wipf & Stock, 2009), p. 77.

4. Cited in Alexandre Kalomiros, *The River of Fire* (Seattle: Saint Nectarios Press, 1980), p. 35.

5. Kalomiros, *The River of Fire*, p. 31.

6. C.S. Lewis, *The Great Divorce* (New York: HarperCollins, 1973), p. 75.

7. "Purgatory," Catholic Answers, www.catholic.com/tracts/purgatory.

8. Luther's letter to Hansen von Rechenberg, cited in Donald G. Bloesch, *The Last Things: Resurrection, Judgment, Glory* (Downers Grove: IVP Academic, 2005), p. 146.

9. Cited in G. Frederick Wright, William G. Ballentine, and Frank H. Foster, eds., *The Bibliotheca Sacra*, vol. 45 (1890, repr., Whitefish: Kessinger, 2010), p. 621.

10. Augustine, *City of God*, book 30, chap. 17.

11. Thomas F. Torrance, "Universalism or Election?" *Scottish Journal of Theology*, 1949, vol. 2, issue 3, pp. 310-18. As I mentioned previously, I am not writing an academic book for scholars but rather a pastoral encouragement for a popular reading audience. If you have an appetite for more robust discussion and are interested in the full debate between Torrance and Robinson, the article from which this quote comes can be purchased in its entirety at journals.cambridge.org/action/displayAbstract?fromPage=online&aid=3282104&fulltextType=RA&fileId=S0036930600004713. The article will be particularly helpful for the Bible student who mistakenly believes that a theology of hope is equivalent to Universalism.

Chapter 9: Seeing Through Agape's Eyes

1. *Grace Walk* was written in 1994 and published by Harvest House Publishers in 1995. At the time of this writing, it has been published in more than a dozen languages around the world.

2. Most Evangelicals would be shocked to know that Paul was actually quoting a 200-year-old poem about Zeus.

> Let us begin with Zeus, whom we mortals never leave unspoken;
> For every street, every market-place is full of Zeus;
> Even the sea and the harbor are full of this deity;
> Everywhere everyone is indebted to Zeus;
> For we are indeed his offspring.

Paul had no problem leveraging the contemporary cultural elements of his day into his presentation of the gospel. It is amazing to see how many ways we can share the gospel when we are free from religious blinders and are captivated by the global grace of God. I once found myself in trouble for quoting rock singer Joe Cocker in a sermon and again another time for quoting singer Jimmy Buffett. Paul didn't seem to have any problem doing such a thing.

3. Maybe a Les lives inside you. Many other verses may come to your mind that would seem to suggest what I've written here isn't true, but each of them has an answer that aligns with the truth of humanity's adoption in Jesus Christ. This book cannot possibly cover all the questions you might have, so visit www.beyondanangrygod.com, where you can dig deeper into this subject than space allows here. I will try to regularly offer additional answers and thoughts on that site.

4. Karl Barth, *Church Dogmatics*, vol. 3 (Peabody: Hendrickson, 2010), p. 613.

5. Norman Grubb, "How Do I Look at People?" *The Intercessor*, Zerubbabel Ministries. Available online at www.zerubbabel.org/newsletter/view_article.asp?ID=901.

6. Robert Capon, *The Romance of the Word: One Man's Love Affair with Theology* (Grand Rapids: Eerdmans, 1996), p. 9.

7. For an interesting personal study on this topic, do an online search of the phrase *objective justification* and see where it takes you. There are many references to this important subject that will take you through church history to see what others have believed about this issue.

8. Thomas Thornburg, *Plato's Republic* (Lincoln: Cliff'sNotes, 1963), pp. 52-53.

9. Steve McVey, *Grace Walk* (1995; repr., Eugene: Harvest House, 2005), pp. 168-69.

More Great Books by Steve McVey
from Harvest House Publishers

52 Lies Heard in Church Every Sunday

Steve shows how pastors and churches can distort scriptural truths because of preconceptions and end up diminishing the loving, personal God who gives the believer everything. As he examines such problems as ignoring part of the truth and confusing our role with God's, Steve guides you to a closer, more fulfilling relationship with Him.

The Secret of Grace

Are you "living by the rules" or letting God's grace rule you? God has provided everything you need for a truly meaningful, joy-filled life here on earth...all because of His marvelous grace. Rest in His grace and let Him live through you. Find out how in *The Secret of Grace*.

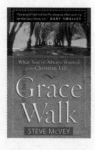

Grace Walk

This bestseller shows you how to leave behind stale, performance-focused, anxiety-ridden Christianity and live the grace walk—the truths of who you are in Christ and how you can experience His life in and through you.

The Grace Walk Devotional

This devotional shows you that God's grace is immensely more than a doctrine. You'll discover why it's all right to give up on yourself and your efforts, who you are in Christ, how to relax and delight in Jesus's love and friendship, and how much He can do through you.

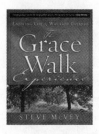

The Grace Walk Experience

This workbook helps you apply eight truths that have changed lives worldwide, understand your identity in Christ, and rest in God's grace.

Grace Walk Moments

Steve invites you to start each day by letting God remind you of His love and care for you. Experience all the grace of God has to offer you—refreshment, joy, and forgiveness—in these quiet moments alone.

Helping Others Overcome Addictions

These addiction-breaking biblical truths will help you help someone—or help you experience freedom yourself. Freedom from addiction comes only when you fully believe what God says about your identity, get radically right with Him, and dwell in your identity in Christ. Material on codependency and implementing recovery/support groups included.

Walking in the Will of God

Helping frustrated Christians rediscover the grace-filled, relational God of the Scriptures, Steve shows you that a rule-focused life causes anxiety and distance from the Father, that a relationship-based life brings security in His dependability, and that believers, knowing God wants to guide them, can relax and enjoy a bold, no-regrets life.

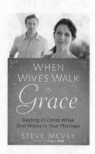

When Wives Walk in Grace

You can't change your husband. Only God can. Steve points you toward how God wants to change you so you can rest in His assurance of your worth, trust and not fret about your husband's spiritual leadership, and see God's bigger picture through specific, attitude-changing steps of faith.

To learn more about Harvest House books and
to read sample chapters, visit our website:

www.harvesthousepublishers.com

HARVEST HOUSE PUBLISHERS
EUGENE, OREGON